Shadows of Survival

A Child's Memoir of the Warsaw Ghetto

JEWS OF POLAND

SERIES EDITOR—**Antony Polonsky**
(Brandeis University)

Shadows of Survival

A Child's Memoir of the Warsaw Ghetto

KRISTINE KEESE

Boston
2016

Library of Congress Cataloging-in-Publication Data:
A catalog record for this book is available
from the Library of Congress.

ISBN 978-1-61811-509-6 (hardback)
ISBN 978-1-61811-510-2 (electronic)
Cover design by Lisa Rosenthal

Book design by Kryon Publishing
www.kryonpublishing.com

Published by Academic Studies Press in 2016
28 Montfern Avenue
Brighton, MA 02135, USA
press@academicstudiespress.com
www. academicstudiespress.com

This book is dedicated to my mother, Eugenia (Genia) Lubowska, Devert (Krolikowska) Krol (1910–1972) and to my uncle, Jakub (Jasio) Lubowski (1915–1979) and to my children, Richard M., Elisabeth K., and Jeffrey C. Rosenthal

Contents

Acknowledgments vii

Introduction.. viii

1. My Personal War.. 1
2. 1939: The Clouds of War..11
3. November 1940–July 1942: The Ghetto, First Stages.................17
4. The Ghetto, Last Stages... 35
5. The End of Safety... 42
6. Jasio's Story and Leaving the Ghetto 50
7. Times of High Anxiety 55
8. August–October 1944: The Warsaw Uprising 76
9. Leaving Warsaw... 88
10. Waiting for the War to End.. 94
11. Spring 1945: Return to the Convent......................................106
12. Living with Genia in Lodz 113

Afterword: What is Left??? 120

Photos and Documents 124

Acknowledgments

This book was written for my children, to whom I wanted to convey the nature of survival and the importance of continuance. Their existence was a source of great pleasure to my mother. They were affected by my experience and by hers in ways we cannot fully know.

In writing this account of my own experiences, I found several sources that help to understand the enormity of these events, based on documented numbers of Jews living in Warsaw in 1939 dead or missing by the end of the war. Chief among these sources were: Wladyslaw Bartoszewski, *The Warsaw Ghetto: A Christian's Testimony* (Boston: Beacon Press, 1987); Yehuda Bauer, *A History of The Holocaust* (New York: Franklin Watts, 1982); Stuart Eizenstat, *Imperfect Justice* (New York: Public Affairs, 2003); Gunnar S. Paulson, *Secret City: The Hidden Jews of Warsaw 1940–1945* (New Haven: Yale University Press, 2002); and Bernard Goldstein, *Five Years in the Warsaw Ghetto* (New York: Doubleday, 1961), first published as *The Stars Bear Witness* (New York: Viking Press, 1949), the best and most detailed description of daily life in the Warsaw Ghetto.

I owe special thanks to Paul Gilmartin, whose sensitive interview, taped in his home in Los Angeles, which became Episode 51 of his program Mental Illness Happy Hour, helped to open a window to my childhood memories.

Most importantly, the events depicted here would have forever remained uncomfortably in the confines of my memory if it were not for the encouragement and invaluable assistance of my oldest friend, Judith Chernaik. As a published author and one who likes to make things happen, having known my mother and the bits and pieces of our story, her conviction that the story should be told, and that I could do it, sustained me through the very painful time of writing, even across continents, as she now lives in London.

I also want to thank my husband, Robert Keese, for his understanding while I retreated into another time and another reality.

Introduction

Coming to Terms with Memories

I have been writing this book for over sixty years, mostly just in my head. As a child in the Warsaw ghetto, I kept a diary interspersed with poems and overheard stories. It had to be destroyed when we left the ghetto so that no traces of where I had been could ever be found.

A year later, during the Warsaw Uprising, I again kept a diary with patriotic songs I had composed, comments, and observations. This also did not survive our escape from the city, for the same reasons. Warsaw residents had been gathered into labor camps—now it would have been equally dangerous to be discovered as a past resident of the no-longer-inhabited city.

Time went on. The war ended. We moved to another country, another life, another culture. The past seemed less and less believable. I was busy with school, work, children. There never seemed to be time to focus on the ever-receding past, or a real desire to do so. If I began to tell my story, I could not stop without wanting to get to the end of it quickly, so it would be over, so I could be sure that I had survived. I made up many arguments for refusing to tell it. Why should I burden others with that history, the increasingly more unbelievable events of my childhood that, for those years, were just my ordinary life? When I first arrived in New York City, at the age of twelve, I felt like one who has just escaped from a lunatic asylum. I did not want others to know of my past lest they would examine me for signs of damage, or even blame.

"I am fine, thank you. I am just like everyone else". Survival had for so long depended on my ability to pass undiscovered. I had been good at it. I wanted to continue my success.

In 1946, at the beginning of my first school year in New York City, one of my eighth-grade classmates asked me questions about the war. When I began to tell some of the story, another interrupted loudly. "Don't believe anything she tells you," she announced. "My father says that all these refugees tell fantastic stories, all lies, so that we feel sorry for them and give them money."

That really shocked me. I was about to defend myself, offer proof, when I thought: *Do I really want to convince my classmates that people did terrible things to other people?* Perhaps it was better that they should not believe me, perhaps that meant that they could not imagine acting like that, so would never be capable of doing it themselves. It seems naïve now, but it made me feel better.

As an adult, I considered that perhaps the reason I could not write this book was that I had no point of view. Was I angry? Was I sad? The story of my individual survival seemed unimportant and not worth telling. The full realization of how tenaciously I resisted revisiting the past dawned on me about twenty years ago, when I was encouraged to register for reparation money offered by the German government. I did not want to register. Asking for reparations seemed like an admission of damage. It would question my survival, my *intact* survival.

"When they get my application," I said to a friend, "they will take out a big ledger and add me to the list of over six million victims. Here is one more, they will say, one that we did not know about." One more victim. I would not give them that satisfaction.

"But surely terrible things must have happened to you," my friend reasoned.

"No," I said. "I was lucky, nothing bad happened to me. I would be compensated for the suffering of others, no longer able to speak for themselves. And anyway, there can be no compensation."

My friend persisted. "Weren't there people close to you who were killed?"

"No," I insisted. But then, I thought for a minute; that sounded crazy. "Oh, yes, I guess. My father and my grandparents and all my friends by the time I was eight years old."

Oh . . . it was just too frightening for me to classify myself as a victim. Victims do not survive. Survival requires constant struggle and vigilance. One cannot afford the luxury of not surviving.

It always seemed to me that survival needs to be practiced and rehearsed. Early in 1942, my mother would manage to cross to the other side of the walled ghetto to sell foodstuffs we were receiving from her husband, my stepfather, who briefly found himself in Brazil. These packages could be delivered because they were shipped from a neutral country. Strange luxuries for the starving inhabitants of the ghetto: coffee, tea, cocoa, sardines, canned pineapple. Things that were coveted by high-end restaurants on the Aryan side. My mother would go to sell them there and brought us bread, potatoes, and sometimes a piece of sausage or eggs, *our* luxuries. When a package arrived, she would announce in the afternoon that she was planning to take it to "the other side." This short notice limited the dire warnings of her brother, my uncle Jasio, and my own choked-down fear. Stopped without a pass and identified as a Jew, she could be summarily shot. My mother was young and attractive, and trusted her luck. She often would be accompanied by her mysterious romantic friend Phillip. Phillip wore a beret and a scarf, and rode a motorcycle. Her friends were suspicious of him. He could seemingly come and go as he pleased. Who was he? How was he able to get his "pass"?

I liked Phillip. Getting into my good graces and buying me treats was his way of courting and annoying my mother. I had no choice but to trust him.

"Don't trust him," Jasio would say. He was my mother's younger brother and lived with us. Jasio's anxiety would cause me to imagine the most unimaginable of disasters: she would not be coming back. But as it got late, Jasio was often not there, spending the night with friends, and I would lie awake in my bed, in the bed my mother and I shared, and try to sleep, waiting for her return. As I waited alone, when the anxiety became unbearable, I would rehearse my survival.

There is a knock on the door, it is someone coming to tell me that my mother has been caught, arrested, or killed. Word of such events always spread quickly among friends. I have to plan exactly what I will do. I will get dressed, put my things together, and go across the courtyard where my best friend Ella Taitelbaum lives with her mother and little sister. I tell them what has happened and Mrs. Taitelbaum says I can come and live with them. I will go back and get my things. I will leave a note for Jasio telling him not to worry about me. I fill this activity with as much detail as I can, so it runs through my mind slowly like a film on a hand-cranked reel. If I really take my time with this fantasy, I will hear my mother's steps on the stairs before I need to start it over.

Years later, when I was first married, my husband's work took him from Boston to New York for two days each month. I drove him to the airport; sometimes on my way back, the familiar feeling of anxiety would seize me. Did the plane make it to New York? How would I find out? The familiar way of rehearsing for disaster could still soothe my anxiety.

I get home and there is a message or a call that tells me of the disaster. I will put together a list of people I should inform. I will begin to make arrangements, sort documents, take care of the children. These plans would keep me calm till I could get home and check on the safe arrival of the plane.

I lost that defense a few years later while staying with friends in Vermont. The children were now four and six. My mother and stepfather were to stop by and pick up the children to take them for a week. It would be a long car ride, and I was concerned about my stepfather's driving. I made sure that the children would sit in the back seat with seatbelts on, but I could not shake off the anxiety. Soon it became intolerable, so I began the narrative that had always soothed me in the past.

OK, now comes the phone call about the accident—what do you do? It did not work. I can do nothing; there is nothing to do. I had no idea it would ever be like that. We had made the usual plans of a young couple with free babysitters, a dinner out, a movie. But I was paralyzed with an irrational grief that I could not share with anyone. I had made the assumption that my children were lost and now I could not go on living. I could not bear the cheerfulness of my friends looking forward to the free evening. I was in another world.

Lest my friends think I was crazy, I announced to everyone that I was suddenly feeling quite sick, perhaps the flu.

"What a shame," they said, "we had such a nice evening planned." They should go ahead and never mind me. "I'll just take a couple of aspirins and go to bed. I am sure it will all be gone by tomorrow."

So they left and I went to bed, and cried and cried, mourning my children. And so, after all those years, I learned that there could be something in my life that I valued above my own survival. That made life a more complex and dangerous journey. It made me realize that it must have been that way for other adults who survived with me, that my existence must have contributed to my mother's will to survive, and she might not have been as brave or as resourceful if it had been only on her own behalf.

Some years later I was asked to translate testimonials collected in Polish from Jewish children newly arrived in Israel, about their experiences in concentration camps, ghettos, and hideouts. This was for research work by a psychiatrist who was interested in the effects of such experiences. It was very difficult for me to read and retype these stories without weeping over the horrors that the children had endured. My children were of school age then, and I was terrified that they might find and read those typewritten pages, so I hid them more carefully than I would have hidden the most graphic pornography. After a while, I refused to read or translate any more of these testimonials.

As my ordinary life went on, I still couldn't bring myself to write my story. Why bring to others what I was trying to get away from myself?

You write to bear witness, they say. A witness to what? To this single event? The horrors of the world kept multiplying around me, while my own experiences receded into the past. There was South Africa. I had recurring nightmares of the Charlottesville Massacre. Then came the Vietnam War. I was there too, huddled in a hut, terrified of those who wanted to kill me for reasons I could neither understand nor prevent. I refused to keep the graphic anti-war posters that my friends hung on their walls. *You may need those to remind you, but I carry those pictures in my head all the time. I don't need to be reminded. I need a space where I can try to forget.*

I studied and taught social science, which has to do with how people behave and why. Yet I did not find the explanations I was searching for. I wrote books and articles, but not about my own experience. The current wars and horrors kept happening. My children were grown and had children of their own. My stories trickled down in partial versions as part of the family history. I still believed that it was better that they should not know the whole story.

But then, quite unexpectedly for me, I too became older. There was no one to ask questions about my memories, no one to fill in the details, and very few were left who shared my experiences. My children were now being entertained by films that depicted parts of my experience. I wanted to know what they were being told. So I went to see *Life is Beautiful* with Robert Benigni. The *New Yorker* published my letter, in which I contested the reviewer's objections to the humor and his disbelief in the story. Survival is always hard to believe, full of strange coincidences and unpredictable events. There is always humor and all the other constant aspects of life, no matter what the circumstances. I went to see *Schindler's List* because my children were going to see it. I also saw *The Pianist*. Some friends were warning me to stay away from that film, as it was too close to my experience. But my Aunt Marysia, who is also a Holocaust survivor, said "Don't worry, you won't see anything you have not seen before."

Afterwards, she asked me, "Do you remember it being so frantic?"

"No," I said, "but this was three years depicted in less than three hours."

Then, I started to think that there would be no one left to tell it all, not just my story, but that of my parents, my grandparents, and my great-grandparents. They are all part of this history. My children would never know what they have inherited, what has been passed on from generation to generation, would not know of their endurance, the twists of their fates, the flow of history that was their world. And there will be no one to honor them. So I am writing this for my children. They are the roots and stock of the living plant. We are just the latest shoots, this one spring's harvest, and maybe at some future time when we stop the killings, maybe then there will be flowers . . . .

The living owe it to those who no longer speak for themselves to tell their story for them

—Czeslaw Milosz

1. My Personal War

I am five years old. We have moved into an apartment where Mietek, my mother's new husband, has always lived with his parents, now deceased. It is the same apartment where my mother had resided for a year in a room rented with two of her friends, when she first came to Warsaw, some ten years previously, to attend the University. It is on the second floor. The front door opens onto an entry hallway, with a coat closet, a small table, and a chair. One door leads to the dining room/living room and another to a study with a large adjoining bedroom. From the dining room, there is an entry to the kitchen with another small bedroom to the side. That is my bedroom. There is a small bureau, a table, and a narrow iron bed, painted white.

That apartment building, at 9 Zlota Street, burned down when the first German bombs fell on Warsaw in 1939. I was with my grandparents in Wloclawek. When we came back to Warsaw, my mother took me to look at the burned-out house and I saw my white iron bed, now mostly turned black, hanging out of my bedroom window, its bottom legs caught on the window ledge. The image of the burned bed is etched in my memory. It is, to me, the symbol of the whole war.

The dining room has a large oval table in the middle. It is covered with a white linen cloth edged with ecru lace. I sat with my grandmother while she made lace like that. Usually, the table is just polished wood. I often sit there tracing letters, trying to teach myself to read. I do that from newspapers that are left lying around, and I find it especially difficult to make what I consider a proper "e," with a straight line across the top and a neat curve around it.

The special tablecloth means that we are expecting company. A smell of freshly baked babka, which Zosia is baking in the kitchen, wafts through the house. It comes to my bedroom first because my room is connected to the kitchen by a small passage that also has a door to the bathroom. The large bedroom on the other side of the entry is where my mother and Mietek sleep. I like having my little bedroom so close to the kitchen. In the morning, when I first wake up, I can slip into the kitchen, absorb all the smells, and stand around the large enamel sink while Zosia puts away the dishes from the night before and makes preparations for the day's housekeeping. Zosia sleeps in an alcove in the back of the kitchen. There is a narrow bed and a chest of drawers; at the opening, a starched cotton drape can be drawn shut to separate it from the rest of the kitchen.

I love the kitchen. Ever since my mother remarried, I am in enemy territory. Every day there are new rules I am told I must obey, such as not talking to my mother when she is resting, because she has frequent headaches. My mother does not belong to me anymore. When Mietek is critical of my behavior, or makes more rules for me to follow, she gets a pained look on her face but she does not interfere. He says I have been spoiled and he is improving my character. I know he hates me. He looks for things that give me pleasure and finds reasons to deprive me of them. My mother was divorced when I was three. In the past two years, I spent a great deal of time with my grandparents or with my mother and Zosia, and weekends with my father.

Zosia has been with us off and on for as long as I can remember. I have an early memory of my mother and Zosia standing at one end of the room, encouraging me to walk toward them. I teeter in their direction and they both extend their arms to catch me. I know it is a genuine memory because I remember a bookcase they stood next to that was huge—I only reached up to the second shelf. The picture of all this is magnified and a bit fuzzy. I was very nearsighted, so that would have been the way I would have seen things around me.

Zosia had come to work for my grandmother as a young peasant girl, when my mother was just a child. She was like a second mother to her, and my grandmother sent her to help my mother in Warsaw when I was born. She is the only one that my mother still listens to since she married Mietek. He does not like that. She often takes my side, but silently. She would not speak out.

I still spend summers with my grandparents, and my father comes most weekends to take me out for part of the day. Those are wonderful times. My father has bought me a blue wool dress with a white collar, just like a dress that Shirley Temple wore in one of her films that he took me to see. I wear the dress every time we go out together. My mother does not like it when he takes me to see films. After I saw *Snow White*, I kept having nightmares and could not sleep. Mietek says I should not be allowed to spend so much time with other family, my grandparents especially, as they spoil me.

My mother and Mietek had married the previous February. My mother and Zosia packed my things, and my uncle Jasio came to take me to my grandparents. We went by train, which was exciting. I was not quite sure what was going on, just that I had to be out of the way. I was told that, when I came back a month later, we would be living in a different house and Mietek would be there all the time.

In my grandparents' house, there was always something for me to do. The whole house was theirs. The square cement block building stood at the back of a narrow walled-in courtyard closed off with a heavy padlocked gate that opened onto the street. The walls on both sides of the courtyard were lined with low wooden sheds. The shed on one side, by the gate, served as an office. The larger shed on the other side was a stable with two horses and a wagon, used to deliver boxes of soap that my grandfather manufactured, as well as a small, light carriage they took out for picnics and rides. The courtyard was paved with cobblestones with a deep rut that ran the length of each side, ending under the gate, so that the whole space could be hosed down. A large doghouse stood by the side of the stable, where their watchdog, let loose at night, would be chained.

The soap factory was the first floor of the main house. A loading platform ran across the front of the house, ending at a set of stairs leading to my grandparents' living quarters on the second floor. On the other side of the stairs was a cement deck covered over with a trellis of grapevines. A large wooden table under the trellis was where we had our meals in good weather. A faint smell of perfumed soap was always in the air.

The factory space was full of vats of dyes, chemicals, and strange mixtures that I had to keep away from. But at the other end, closer to

3

the doors to the loading dock, was the equipment that stamped out blocks of soap. I was allowed to stand by that end and watch pink and blue squares of soap tumble down to be stamped at the final step with a figure of a young dancer in regional costume from the Polish region of Kujawy: a *Kujawianka*. That was the trade name of my grandfather's soap. Finally, the small squares of soap were packaged in colorful boxes decorated with a picture of the dancing *Kujawianka* and the address and name of the manufacturer.

Since my grandfather was present at all meals, the household revolved around these preparations. When I was there, the focus was on what I liked or what they thought I should be eating. Every other morning the milkman came, pushing a hand cart with vats of milk, cream, and sour cream, a big part of Polish cooking. These would be ladled out with a long-handled ladle into containers that my grandmother Babusia brought down to him. In the summer, he also carried baskets of berries: strawberries, blueberries, and currants, which his family members had picked that morning. Sometimes, there would be mushrooms brought in from the woods, probably picked by the children in the family. In Poland, gathering mushrooms is often a task for small children. Poisonous mushrooms are so easily recognized that there is little danger of a mistake.

The house had an attic where my grandmother kept a few chickens. There was no room for more than four or five, as they had to be kept in enclosures to protect them from rats. There were also white pigeons that nested in the rafters. So we had fresh eggs as well as chicken soup, and occasionally my grandmother would make pigeon soup, just for me, which was a great delicacy. I loved to go up to the attic and feed the chickens and watch the pigeons fly in and out, though I tried not to think of them when soup was served.

Although my photos from those times show a round-faced, pudgy little girl, my grandmother always thought I should be eating more. She had my favorite dishes prepared and still coaxed and bribed me to eat. I did not like drinking milk, which had to be boiled and was always hot. A box of chocolates in different animal shapes contained the milk bribes. She would drop a chocolate creature into my hot milk, and

I would try to drink it fast enough to still identify the animal before it melted away. There was a small, pretty jam spoon for scraping the melted chocolate out of the bottom of the cup.

If the dish was not so well liked, but something she thought I should eat, there were also scare tactics. For that she would conscript my grandfather. After I was told that there was a monster in the closet who was upset because I would not take three more bites of whatever it was, my grandfather would emerge with a heavy coat over his head, and in a threatening gruff voice tell me I must eat them or else . . . Surely I knew it was him, my very beloved Dziadzius, and yet, there was always an edge of doubt, a small fear of a possible unknown, *what if* . . . .

My grandfather was the one adult in my childhood whom I loved unreservedly, the one adult into whose lap I could always climb and know I was welcome. He was a tall, handsome man with a full head of white, silky hair. After supper, sitting in his lap, I would take a comb and run it through his hair, changing the part to make him look funny, then returning him to a perfect look. I can easily recall the feel of his hair and the smell of his jacket as I tucked my face into his shoulder, a mixture of the soap he manufactured and the tobacco he smoked in his pipe.

I had learned that refusing to eat was the only way one could stand up to an adult, or refusing to get out of bed, but that was to be used as a last resort. Later, I learned that those things only had an effect on adults who cared.

Mietek did not mind sending me to my room with no supper, glad to be rid of my presence. That much I soon guessed. I felt that he hated me, but it was not till I was an adult that I understood his character and the circumstances that led to that hatred.

But I also found out that to understand is not the same as to forgive.

That year, the summer following the marriage, Mietek vetoed my usual stay at my grandparents. He found a children's camp where I could spend the summer without being a favored child and so begin to "build my character." He and my mother took me by train, and then a horse cab from the station, to a large house in the country surrounded by woods. The property was enclosed by a tall wrought-iron fence and gate. I was five years old.

My mother was obviously concerned about leaving me with strangers. She lingered as I clung to her, not quite believing that she would actually leave. Finally, protesting tearfully, I was sternly led away by one of the caretakers. I saw my mother glance back with a confused look. I broke away from the woman restraining me and ran to the fence, only to see my mother disappearing from view. Grasping the wrought iron fence, I screamed and kicked until, defeated and worn out, I was led away. My things and I were put into a room with several cots in it and I was sat down at a long wooden table with other children. It was suppertime. I think I was the youngest child there. I have always been rather tall for my age, but I remember being the smallest when we lined up.

I cried myself to sleep that night and the next day refused to eat any breakfast.

During the day, we went for walks in the woods and games were organized. I did not know any of the games; in fact, I did not know how to play. At home, I usually spent time by myself or with adults. I was clumsy and not very outgoing, and it was a few years before it was discovered that I was very nearsighted, something I inherited from my father. But I liked going out into the woods. There, I usually sat by myself away from the other children, looking closely at flowers and insects that I could then see better, crying a little, but comforted by the plants around me and the smells of the woods. I was left alone since I was not being a bother to anyone.

The evening after my first day, my mother telephoned to ask how I was doing. When I was called to the phone and heard her voice, I became so hysterical and wept so violently that the receiver was yanked from my hand. She was asked not to call again until I had some time to adjust. Hearing them say she was not to call threw me into deeper despair.

I still refused to eat. This time it was not a ruse; I could not swallow a bite.

A decision was made to force me to eat. After the other children had finished their food and left the dining room, I was told to stay. As I sat over an untouched plate, one of the adults sat next to me and forced me to swallow, spoonful after spoonful. As the food mixed with tears in my throat, I gagged on my sobs and finally threw up all the forced food. It was cleaned up and I was put to bed.

The next morning, a different strategy must have been decided on to break what they considered my "stubbornness." Again, I was forced to eat after all the children had left. I will never forget that meal. It was oatmeal and the husks left on the flakes irritated my already raw throat. I threw up, but this time, the caretaker held a bowl under my chin and coolly made me eat again what I had just regurgitated. I can vividly recall all the feelings that went with that event, but I have no memory of how it ended or what happened the rest of that day. I am sure I was in hysterics. I don't remember ever eating a meal at that place. I don't know how many days I was there. It could not have been many.

I just remember the morning when they packed my things and led me to the gate. And there was the most wonderful sight. It was my grandfather's carriage with his driver, who was handed my suitcase. I was lifted up and deposited on my grandmother's lap, while Zosia, who sat next to her, started smoothing my hair, saying how thin I looked.

"No wonder they refused to be responsible any longer," my grandmother said. "She could have gotten sick. Imagine sending her off like that—what were they thinking?"

Was anyone ever told that I was made to eat the food I threw up? I doubt it. I never told.

I spent the rest of that summer at my grandparents. It was the last summer before the oncoming war overshadowed all else. I remember eating wild strawberries with sweetened fresh cream, a chicken soup my grandmother made with one of the attic chickens, whose insides contained potential eggs, of all different sizes. Small round yolks floated about in the delicious broth. For dessert, there would be Zosia's wonderful honey cake and gingerbread.

When the summer was over and I returned to Warsaw, Mietek decided to hire a governess for me who would come in the mornings to help me dress and comb my hair and take me out for a walk. All the things my mother used to do with me. I was also to enter kindergarten that fall. Thus battle lines were redrawn.

Combing my hair in the mornings was always a bit of a production. My hair was long, and fell below my waist. It had never been cut and since I was not a particularly pretty little girl, I was well aware that my hair was the one thing that drew admiration. It was fine and knotted easily and the morning comb-out was difficult. I would often scream in pain as the knots were tugged on. It was in fact painful, but it was also satisfying when my mother expressed concern over my discomfort and was especially careful not to pull my hair, combing it out carefully. The hired governess, probably trying to do her best, was not able to pacify me easily. One morning, as I was objecting loudly to the yanking of my hair, Mietek rushed in and told me harshly to be quiet because my mother had a headache and was lying down. I expected that my cries would bring her to my side. I knew she must have wanted to come in and help, but Mietek stopped her, determined that I would not be "spoiled." This was the last straw. As he was telling me to be quiet, I said, "This is my room and I will scream as loudly as I want." I could see him start to go into a rage, but I knew he would not hit me.

"Then you can stay in your room all week," he said, "And don't let me find you in any other part of the house."

I could go outside with my governess but all my meals were served in my room. The particularly onerous part of that for me was not being able to go into the kitchen, where Zosia would let me help her cook and lick out the pots with left-over delicacies. Raw babka dough made with yeast and raisins was my favorite. There, I always felt welcome and cared for. I don't know how long this exile actually lasted, but I was aware that it created tension between my mother and Mietek, leaving me with a combined sense of guilt and satisfied revenge.

I had more than one governess through the first few months of that year. I can't remember any of them, but I became very adept at having them fired. Knowing how easily Mietek became irritated by any infraction of what he considered proper behavior, I found ways to blame these young strangers for anything he did not like. If he disapproved of what I was wearing, they made me put it on despite my objections. I implied that they had made disparaging remarks about him or other members of the family. I accused them of various minor transgressions of cleanliness, stupidity, or forgetfulness, anything I could think of that would earn his disapproval. I think I was helped by the fact that they did not like the job or me anyway, and that my mother was not totally convinced they should be there and was glad of an excuse to let them go.

I remember two other disciplinary issues with Mietek. It appeared that I was afraid of heights, something that is with me to this very day. But I think as a child it was caused by the fact that I was so nearsighted that distance from the ground was difficult for me to judge and made the ground and the steps below me look unreachable. Mietek set up a stepladder in the bathroom that I had to climb every morning before breakfast, until my head touched the ceiling. It did not cure me of my fear of heights, as I climbed crying and trembling, feeling dizzy and nauseated. But I never forgot the fear, the humiliation and anger. All compounded by the perception of my mother's discomfort and her inability to defend me. She was being convinced that it was for my own good and would develop strength of character that she was denying me, and there was the need to present a united parental front. I felt her helplessness as well as mine.

There was one event, though, that worked out well. One day, a friend of Mietek's came to visit with an enormous St Bernard. I was terrified. That convinced Mietek to get a dog to help me overcome my fear. But the dog they got, which was to be a large German shepherd, was a small puppy when it came and I loved it. It was, in fact, from my grandparents' house. Their female watchdog had mated with a wolf that came in the night from the nearby woods. Given its mixed heritage, the puppy was difficult to housebreak and threatening to strangers, delivery people, and postmen. They named the dog Phillip and I was thrilled to have him in the house. Perhaps having another transgressor in the house helped, plus the fact that this was a threatening dog to others but was my friend. Long after he was no longer with us, Phillip stayed in my night dreams and in my daydreams to represent a force I could rely on, a defender.

The year was 1939, the war was looming, and Mietek was called up as a reservist in the anti-artillery air force. When he left on his assigned motorcycle, in uniform and undoubtedly glamorous, I was already with my grandparents for the summer, where I stayed when the war broke out on September 1st of that year. I did not see him again for seven years and have often wondered how my sanity would have been damaged if he had been there all along.

Many times, after we were reunited with Mietek and lived for some years uncomfortably together, my mother tried to convince me that he was really a loving person who did not know how to express his feelings. It was not until shortly before she died that she was able to say to me, "I made a terrible mistake. I mistook lack of heart for strength of character."

2. 1939: The Clouds of War

It was the late summer of 1939. Adults spent much time listening to the radio; there were long speeches that no conversation would be allowed to interrupt. Mietek's engineer friends, when they came to visit, spoke about the marvels of German technology. Many had previously studied in German universities. Germany was in everyone's conversation. Mietek spent his evenings at the dining room table discussing with my mother the letters he was writing to foreign companies, applying for work in exotic-sounding countries. He was a metallurgical engineer and was looking for work in South America, where mining was booming.

I had started going to preschool and was chosen to play Red Riding Hood, mainly on account of my long hair, and our dog Phillip was to be the Big Bad Wolf. At the last minute, though, it turned out that I was too tongue-tied to say my lines and the other children were frightened by the dog, so it did not work out. When school was out, I went as usual to stay with my grandparents. There, too, the atmosphere was tense. Most evenings my grandparents sat by their radio, listening to the booming broadcasts. The word "war" was ever present. I tried to puzzle out what it meant. I had a vivid dream one night: all the people in the town were lined up on one side of the street and across the street was a line of strangers. They glared at each other with hatred. That was my image of war, the image came up whenever I heard the word. The tension and the worry increased. We no longer had picnics in the woods, and the fear and uncertainty were constant. I was at my grandparents' house when the war broke out.

Then, one night, I was briefly awakened as I was being carried out of my bed by my grandfather. Still wrapped in blankets, I was tucked inside our soap delivery wagon. There were bundles of our belongings around me and soon the rattling of the wagon over the cobblestones put me back to sleep. I woke up suddenly when the motion stopped.

We were in a long line of wagons strung along the country road. It was a very dark night—there were stars, but no lights in any of the buildings. A monster with a long snout and huge eyes leaned over me, just like some horrible version of the Big Bad Wolf. I was terrified, but seeing me he moved aside the long nose and said something reassuring. It was a Polish soldier wearing a gas mask. I had seen gas masks before but never actually on someone. There were many voices clamoring that they wanted to get to Warsaw. We were ordered to turn around and go home. Warsaw was under heavy bombardment and not safe at all. It took a lot of convincing to give up the idea that Warsaw, the capital, was not the safest place to be. By morning, I was back in my own bed, and the whole night's adventure seemed like a bad dream.

The days that followed were doubly tense. Poland had fallen quickly; the army was disbanded. No Germans had come to Wloclawek yet, so there was no fighting and no defense. There was no news of my mother and no way to get information. A few days after our curtailed attempt to get to Warsaw, a horse-drawn wagon pulled into the courtyard and there was my mother with just a suitcase in hand, a shawl over her head, and she was weeping.

"Is it Mietek?" my grandmother asked. "Is he dead?"

"No, no," she said. "I've had no news of him, but Phillip, the dog, I had to give him away," and she broke into a torrent of tears, hardly able to speak.

She finally told us the whole story. Our house in Warsaw was one of the first to be destroyed in the heavy bombing. It was all over very soon; the Polish defenses could not withstand the airpower. Poland capitulated and able-bodied inhabitants of the city were set to work cleaning up the debris. While our building was on fire, our dog had disappeared in the commotion. But later, when all was quiet again, she ran into an acquaintance who told her that her dog was lying among the ruins of her old building, half starved and hurt, but he would not go with anyone, even people he knew. She went right over and there was Phillip. It looked like he had been shot in the leg, but it was a superficial wound and was already healing. She took him with her and gave him what food she could find, and then discovered the problem.

Walking down the street, the sight of a German soldier in uniform would drive him to fury—it was all she could do to keep him from attacking. She surmised that he must have been wounded by a German in uniform, and from now on he was a danger to her.

She was coming to Wloclawek anyway to get me, and she now had to leave the city with the dog. She bought what food she could to feed him, then was able to pay her way from town to town towards Wloclawek. Shortly before she arrived, she saw a farmer working in the fields and asked if he would like a watchdog. She made the farmer promise that he would treat him well and let her take him back when it was all over. She explained the problem, fed him the last of the food she had, and left.

It was quite some time before she stopped mourning that separation. I sensed that her mother and father were disapproving, that in all this uncertainty about the survival of her husband, her child, and her brother, she suffered so over the separation from her dog.

Not long after that, we found some transportation to return to Warsaw. There must have been reasons, which I was not aware of, for us to hurry back. Warsaw had a special status under the occupation; it was not to be incorporated into the Third Reich, as was the region of Wloclawek, closer to Germany. All this I know from subsequent history. I was not in Wloclawek when the Germans came in and only heard of the atrocities committed shortly after that occupation, especially the treatment of Jews. We were back in Warsaw by then, first staying with a friend of my mother's, sharing her room, then finding a room to rent near our old neighborhood near the center of town.

The first days, or maybe weeks, following our return were taken up by the paperwork that the German occupying authorities demanded. All residents had to register and collect their birth certificates, medical documents, and the like. Jews were to declare themselves in a separate registry, as the latest Polish passports no longer listed religious affiliation. All those lists had a seemingly benign purpose, to register for housing, for food rations, for medical care, to find relatives and legitimate work. It was considered an expression of the German sense of order and organization that had long been admired.

I do not remember much of that time. It seemed that Genia, my mother, was always very busy. I was alone a lot. Being in a shared apartment, I had to be quiet and stay in one place. I made only one friend. She would come over to my house and we would play doctor, and when assured of privacy had the occasional thrill of taking turns ordering each other to remove our underpants and examine our private parts. There was the pleasure of feeling guilty and scared. I felt estranged from the other children in the neighborhood. My favorite fantasy was that I would get Phillip back and walk him down the street and frighten the other children, who would then understand that I was more powerful than they thought.

My mother received news through the Red Cross that Mietek was alive. As a lieutenant in an anti-artillery division, he had transportation, a motorcycle. After Poland capitulated and the army was officially disbanded, he gathered his men and told them that they could go back home or stay with him and they would try to make their way west, to the still-active front lines and keep fighting. Some did that. And so they went on to Hungary, and eventually to Italy.

He and Genia had friends in Switzerland; all through the war, they communicated by writing to that neutral country and having the letters transferred to wherever they were.

Eventually, Mietek and some of his division made their way to Italy. Through some professional and social contacts he made in the army, he attempted to arrange our transit to Italy. And so, one day a uniformed guard from the Italian embassy knocked on our door and delivered a letter to my mother stating that the queen of Italy (Italy still had a court then) was inquiring about the well-being of the wife of Engineer J. M. Krol. My mother jumped into action; this was an amazing opportunity. Perhaps Mietek had written to advise her how to proceed. She made an appointment at the Italian embassy and applied for a visa. On the strength of the official letter, she managed to convince the secretary that there was interest in the upper echelon of the Italian court in her fate. Soon there were papers to fill out, one of which had to be proof of Aryan origins. She had to be a Christian. Such documents could be purchased for a high price if one knew the right people.

Genia did not have the money nor did she trust those channels. She went to a local church and presented the priest with her dilemma. She was born, she told him, in the eastern part of Poland, which was now under Russian occupation. All her documents had been destroyed when her house in Warsaw was burned. Now she had an opportunity to go to Italy to join her husband, but she had no documents to certify her Christian origins. Perhaps the Good Father would consider doing her the favor of writing a certificate saying that he had known her for years and could attest to her Aryan origins. If he did so, she and her child would be able to join her husband and perhaps escape the war.

Yes, he agreed, he could not write in Italian but he would write it in Latin. She asked what she could do in return; the priest said to just drop a contribution into the poor box on her way out. Her quandary, she always said in telling the story, was how much money to give, worried that too much would be suspicious, too little would seem ungrateful.

With this crucial document, the visa application was completed. The approval and arrangements required several trips to the Gestapo office. It was during those trips that there was another incident that she reported to her friends with great amusement. While in the Gestapo office, being interviewed by a young lieutenant, she was nervously twisting a string of pearls she wore, the string broke and the beads scattered on the floor. As she bent down to try to gather them, the young Gestapo officer gallantly got on his hands and knees and helped her to collect the broken necklace. I think that eased the tension—after that, there was no question that all documents would be approved. Of course, the very application was proof of both her Aryan origins and cosmopolitan interests. This little bit of male–female interplay has always stuck in my mind, as have other moments of humanity breaking through the rigidities of war.

It was necessary to obtain a list of possessions that we would be allowed to take out of the country. The document from the Gestapo listed all personal items for her and for me, down to the number of handkerchiefs and underpants. Again, that German sense of order. The final exit documents had to be processed and approved by the German Headquarters in Crakow, a train ride out of the jurisdiction of Warsaw. That presented a new danger. Germany needed laborers, thus it was not uncommon for a street to be closed and able-bodied people gathered into trucks and sent to labor in Germany. Usually, there were warnings and the possibility of escape from those street collections. But trains were especially dangerous. There were many incidents of trains being stopped and all passengers detained as potential laborers to be shipped to Germany. Genia wanted to go herself to Cracow to get the documents approved, but her friends managed to dissuade her.

These overheard arguments in which I had no say added to my general sense of uncertainty. It would be an awful chance to take; she could lose everything. In the end, she was convinced not to go and instead to hand the documents to a travel bureau that would process them and return them to her all properly stamped. To her dismay, the day after she handed the documents over, there were some irregularities discovered in the travel bureau's dealings and it was temporarily shut down for an investigation. She was furious at being talked out of going herself. There was nothing to do but wait.

In the meantime, two train tickets to Milan arrived in the mail; we used the time to assemble the articles of clothing we were allowed to take with us. The political front was shifting; would it still be safe to travel? It was a little over two weeks before the travel bureau finally reopened; our documents were ready in Warsaw, all approved. But the very day before, Italy declared war, joining the Axis, and the borders were closed. So ended the prospect of leaving Poland.

As the political winds were changing, Mietek had already left and gone on to France. As he told us later, he had hired a taxi to meet every train that arrived from Warsaw to Milan, with directives to take us immediately to a train for Paris, and two tickets waiting. I have often considered that our chances of survival would not have been very good in countries where we did not know the language and had no friends, countries that were eventually conquered by Germany and where the Jews fared no better. Strange quirk of fate. My mother preserved the two tickets to Milan for years.

3. November 1940– July 1942: The Ghetto, First Stages

In Warsaw, an ordinance was issued that all Jews must move to designated sections of Warsaw. The relocations were to be completed by mid-November. They included much of the traditional Jewish section, later to be referred to as the "large ghetto." Those like my family and most of the people we knew, to whom being Jewish was not a conscious functional part of their identity and who were assimilated into all parts of the city, were now scrambling for a place to live. As the area to be included in the ghetto was increased in size, another section of the city was added, one that included a more middle-class neighborhood of Warsaw. This was referred to as the "small ghetto"; the two sections were linked by an overpass across a major city thoroughfare.

The "small ghetto" was where my aunt Cesia and her husband already had a permanent apartment. They were both doctors and lived there with their son, who was just finishing medical school, Aunt Cesia, who was my grandmother's youngest sister (so actually my mother's aunt) and her husband, Uncle Peter, referred to themselves as socialists and were devoted members of the Esperanto movement. Esperanto was based on the Spanish language and the idealistic hope that if everyone in the world had a common language, it would bring universal peace. They spoke Spanish fluently. They had emigrated to South America in the early 1930s and had lived in Rio de Janeiro. By some odd decision, maybe motivated by a concern for the rest of their extended family, they chose to return to Poland in the spring of 1939. It was said in the family that Aunt Cesia became homesick and wanted to come back. In the end, she was the only one to survive that return.

For those who had to move in or out of the designated Jewish section, the scramble to find an apartment was all-consuming. During much of that time, I stayed with Aunt Cesia, but there was no room for all of us. Eventually, Genia found a room in a house nearby, in an apartment occupied by a young couple. Their extra bedroom became our quarters: myself, my mother, and Jasio. We all shared the bathroom and the kitchen. It was close enough to Aunt Cesia's for us to have dinner there often. Later, I could walk to Aunt Cesia's apartment and back by myself, when streets were still safe and life seemed normal. They had a kitchen with a big icebox refrigerator, and there was still ice delivered to them every few days. They also had a pair of small turtles that they had brought with them from South America. The turtles spent most of their time in a shoebox under the family bed, and I could coax them out with bits of food, green vegetables mainly. Perhaps it was hibernation time. I mainly remember feeding them asparagus and rhubarb. I was fascinated by the way they would clamp their sharp, but toothless, jaws on those stringy foods and draw off the solid stalk, till only the strings were left.

Things at Cesia's house were still comparatively normal. Sometimes all of us would have dinner together, with Jasio, who was close to the age of Cesia's son David, teasing each other or the two of them playing jokes on me. My weakness was food—once, they talked me into wanting to taste spicy mustard, which was unknown to me and which they pretended was delicious. They put a large tablespoon of it in my mouth and had much fun with my discomfort. It served me right, they said, to my tears, for being greedy. There was a phonograph in the house. Aunt Cesia and Uncle Peter played classical music; he was an accomplished violinist, while their son, David, had a singing dog. An Irish setter that could be coaxed to whine in tune with popular songs.

Those evenings at Aunt Cesia's were the most I remember of normal touches of family life in Warsaw during the war. It could not have lasted very long, but in those days everything seemed very temporary and nothing was expected to last.

Eventually, our move was completed to a room Genia was able to sublet in a second-story apartment on nearby Ceglana Street. We took all our belongings there and stored some in the building's basement. All these moves were made on the assumption that all arrangements were temporary, for the hopefully short duration of the war. It was always just a matter of getting by.

The building we now lived in, in the assigned ghetto section, was a typical older two-story apartment building with four sides, set around a square courtyard. It was entered from the street by a narrow, dark corridor that opened up into the courtyard, from which several entrances led to separate staircases and sets of apartments. There was a tall acacia tree in the middle, still covered this late spring with pale-purple flowers. A small bordered square under the tree must have been used once as a children's sandbox, now filled with a mixture of sand and dirt. The back side of the building, which was only one story high, bordered an outdoor space with a couple of jasmine bushes with fragrant white flowers. The bushes, leaning against a low wooden fence, created an unexpected oasis from the asphalt courtyard and the gray street beyond. This space framed an entrance to a large door that led to the café. A couple of tables could be set out in good weather. The café door opened onto a large room with more tables and a stage in front for performers; it was really a sort of nightclub. Evenings, not late as there was a curfew, there was often music or a stage show.

Shortly after we moved there, my mother was happily bustling around the café, waiting on tables. Perhaps she had already secured the job before we moved. I was so used to her managing, whatever the circumstances, that it seemed natural that she would have a place where she could work and keep an eye on me. The café was open late afternoon through evening; I had the run of both the indoor and the outside courtyard. In the beginning, when streets were still safe in the daytime, I went every night to Cesia's house for dinner, walking there and back. Later, when walking down the street was no longer safe, all I had to do was to go upstairs to eat the dinner Genia had prepared for me, and eventually put myself to bed.

Our private space was just one room, a back bedroom. We shared the kitchen, which functioned at first, though within a year there was

19

no longer either gas or electricity. We then had a small coal stove for heat and cooking in our room. One had to cross a small living room and enter the adjoining bedroom, which was ours. The room was where the three of us lived, my mother Genia, myself, and Jasio. We had two beds. I shared one with my mother. Two chairs, a small table, and the small coal stove pretty much filled the room.

There was not much space for the three of us. Jasio and I often got into fights that my mother had to arbitrate. He was a handsome young man who loved to tell jokes and tease me, often to amuse young women acquaintances. Our main fights were about privacy. He would have a visitor while I hung around curious, and he'd ask me to close the door. When I went to do that, he would say, "I meant on the other side," and shove me out, locking the door behind me. I would run complaining of the insult to my mother. So, eventually I spent much of my time outside in the courtyard or by the café. There were many other children from our crowded building and nearby apartments who spent their days in that courtyard.

In 2012, I saw a German film, only recently found in German archives, which depicted life in the Warsaw ghetto. It was to show how well Jews were treated. Besides many staged scenes of opulent dinners and rich Jews, there was a shot of women sunbathing on the flat roof of our building. When I first saw the building, I experienced a purely physical reaction of sudden terror, although I did not immediately recognize the building. It was smaller than I would have thought, and shabbier. It was only the churning of my stomach that caught my attention; then, slowly, I remembered the details of the windows and the event, when women were asked to pose as sunbathers in their bathing suits. Some refused while others must have been frightened or bribed into agreeing. I remembered seeing them on the roof from my own window opposite.

When we first moved to this building, the courtyard was something of a shock. The children were different from the well-behaved offspring of my parents' friends, with whom I had occasionally played, or the classmates in the kindergarten I briefly attended before the war. They were different even from the courtyard playmates in the apartment house we had roomed in right after our return to Warsaw, before we moved to the ghetto. I found myself surrounded by a loud, aggressive group of kids of various ages who looked unkempt and unfriendly. Those were the children I walked by on the poorest streets of Warsaw. To my horror, I realized they were all Jewish. Before I even had the chance to go upstairs, a fat little girl with kinky dark hair started to punch me. I can't remember what started it. I must have seemed strange to them, too, and uppity. I had never been in a physical fight. Name-calling came more easily to me than hitting; while Jasio, who was moving our stuff upstairs, stopped to see what was going on, I called her a "dirty Jewish cow." I don't know where the words had come from, but Jasio came flying downstairs, grabbed me, and said I must not talk like that. I had never seen him so angry at me.

"Why not?" I asked. "That's what she is."

Jasio said, "Because you are Jewish, too."

I was horrified. How could I not have known this? I never considered myself as one of those people. Through all the conversations I was overhearing, and the move, I somehow managed not to let it be about me, not part of my life. Jasio dragged me upstairs and lectured me on how to fit in. I listened, but I knew better. I was not one of those people. I was not like them. I would not share their fate.

In the end, I made one friend, Ella Taitelbaum. She was my age, and she lived with her mother and younger sister Muha ("*Muha*" was her nickname, meaning housefly or, actually, a pest) in one of the basement apartments. Her mother was home all the time and so became our caretaker, sharing with me the food she made for her daughters. Ella and I discovered there was a library nearby we could walk to, and we signed up to take out books. The children's section did not have many books available, so we got permission slips from our mothers to take books from the adult section. I read about a book a day, swallowed them, my mother used to say. Once I picked up a book, I could hardly be parted from it till I finished it. I took out any book that had the word "adventure" in the title; that is how I happened to read Andre Gide's *Lafcadio's Adventures*, coming upon it years later and marveling that I still remembered twists of the plot, though I had little idea of what it was about. I read Kipling and all of Karl May's "Cowboys and

Indians" stories. Karl May's book was responsible for my failing in one of the small duties assigned to me in my family. Genia would prepare dinner before she left for work and leave a pot on the coal stove to stay warm. I was to take care of it till Jasio came home. I spent that time reading. As we no longer had electricity, I had to stop reading when the light failed, so I would move my chair closer and closer to the window to catch the last rays of light. By the time Jasio came home, I was sitting at the open window, leaning out and holding my open book as far out as I could reach, the words barely visible, hurrying to the end of the chapter. When Jasio came in, yelling at me, I had little idea of where I was, but I suddenly became aware that the house was filled with smoke. His dinner, which started as a stew with potatoes and onions, was just bits of charcoal. He was hungry and upset.

"How could you do this?" he raged at me. "Didn't you smell the smoke?"

Of course, I smelled the smoke and it bothered my eyes. I did what I thought would help so I could continue reading. "I smelled it," I said. "I opened the window."

It was a long time before Jasio or my mother let me forget this incident.

A short time later, Ella and I decided to organize a school for the small children in the courtyard. We asked children to assemble at nine in the morning on their doorsteps. The parents, glad to have us babysitting, provided us with paper and pencils, and we set up the task of teaching the alphabet and numbers to four- and five-year-olds. We were very bossy and demanding teachers. I am not sure how long this project lasted. Nothing in the ghetto seemed to last very long—I remember these events as short chapters in my life. The situation in the ghetto was constantly changing; when I think back on it now, it is like a kaleidoscope. Each stretch of time we settled into seemed that it would be our life from then on, but it always changed quickly and the transitions came so suddenly and were so fraught with fear that it is hard to remember them.

Marek was my other courtyard friend, whom I met shortly after we moved in. After that first experience with the courtyard kids, I pretty much kept away from everyone, and no one bothered much with me. I was no fun. But one day when I came out, I saw that a large group had surrounded a boy I had never seen before. After grabbing his cap, they threw it around the circle. The one who caught it would pretend to give it back to him and pitch it away as soon as it was within his reach. A time-honored game with which to tease a new kid.

He did not seem to be enjoying the game and was near tears in frustration. I joined in, to everyone's surprise, and when the cap was thrown my way, I caught it and returned it to its owner. A spoilsport, just what everyone expected of me.

He came back later that day. We sat down to talk and he became a daily visitor. This was still at a time when I walked to Aunt Cesia's house for dinner with her and Uncle Peter. Marek would walk with me the few blocks to where they lived. I was eight and he was twelve. He knew a lot about the stars—when it got dark, he would point them out to me and tell me their names. He wanted us to go to other places, and promised to show me strange things that were going on in the neighborhood, but I was not ready to venture much beyond my allowed routes.

One night, he met me as I was coming back. It was getting dark and he said he wanted to show me something. We walked a couple of blocks out of our way and I heard a strange sound coming from an open upper-story window of a house.

Framed in the light was a woman holding a baby. She was keening loudly. I realized I had heard the sound from a distance on previous nights.

"The boys have been coming here for a couple of nights," Marek said excitedly. (The "boys" were street kids he hung out with.) "The baby is dead. She cries and then after a while she drops it."

I froze. "But then she comes out, picks it up and takes it back," he said. "It's been three days."

I hurried home. I told no one about it. I was angry with Marek for taking me there. The picture of the woman framed in the window with the baby in her arms and the weeping sound she made has stayed with me forever.

I never knew where Marek lived or with whom. It was as if every individual were surrounded by an invisible barrier beyond which it was

23

not a good idea to look. We must have considered our present as very discontinuous, unreal, so difficult to understand and, most of all, always temporary.

Would not the war be over soon and life be normal again? The present was just something to get by and survive.

Marek's plan was to be an architect. He promised to build me a house. We often sat on the abandoned sandbox, where he drew plans with a broken tree branch and explained how the construction would proceed. Or, as it got dark, he would draw the constellations of the stars and tell me what they were called. He liked it when I did not know things and he could teach me.

One day, he asked: "Do you know how babies are made?" I said I did, so he quizzed me on it, which embarrassed me. I was pretty sure I knew. He wanted to know what names I called the parts of the body that were involved. I was too shy to say. These were words I had only used with my mother. So he asked me to write the names in the sand, and when I did he laughed and said that these were baby-names, that grownups had other words.

And what about the act itself, what was that called? I didn't know. I felt really stupid.

"Haven't you ever seen those words written on the walls along the street?"

"No, I never noticed."

"So today," he said, "when you go to your aunt's house, look around, tell me tomorrow and I will explain what they mean." Usually, I just wanted to get there as fast as I could and would never stop to look at a wall. This time, I carefully looked round me. Nothing, I saw nothing. A name here and there, some scribbles, but nothing I could identify as an unfamiliar word.

The next morning, Marek was waiting for me. "What did you see?"

"Nothing, there was nothing."

He was annoyed with me. "Did you look?"

"Yes," I said. "I looked everywhere along the way. There was nothing."

"But did you look on your way back?"

Of course, I had not looked on my way back. I realized from his disappointed reaction that he must have followed behind me, scribbling on walls.

Despite this failed attempt at my education, he was not ready to give up on my lessons, so he just wrote the words out for me in the sand. I recognized them. They were forbidden words, used by people who scared me. Words I had heard, just never thought I needed to know.

A few days later, Marek told me that some of the girls and boys from the building were meeting in the basement and doing "it." Would I consider it, with him? I was tempted—everything we did together was fun. I hated to say no to him, so I said I would think about it and let him know.

And I did think about it, a lot. Up to that time, I could share everything with my mother. I somehow felt this was something I could not tell her, though I was not sure why.

So when a few days later Marek asked me again (I had managed to avoid him for a day or so), I said, "No, I would not, because I did not think my mother would like it." We did not speak of it again.

The café where my mother worked also played a major role in my life in the building. There were magic shows, and a few times the magician would ask my mother to let me come in and be his assistant. I experienced that mixture of horror and excitement and pride that must be what every shy person goes through when suddenly in an envious position of receiving full attention. Anyway, I guess I liked it, and tried to figure out in vain how suddenly a coin or a scarf would be pulled out of my ear while I felt nothing.

My mother's friend Phillip would come by on a motorcycle to sit in the café. Phillip was tall and dark and wore a jaunty cap, and would take my mother off sometimes in the evening, to Jasio's great disapproval. I liked him and he liked me, and once teased my mother by inviting me to have tea and pastries with him at the café table while she waited on us. As is the fashion in European cafés, a large tray of pastries would be set in front of us and later the server would count how many were missing to charge accordingly.

25

I was known in the family for having a sweet tooth, and I was always hungry anyway. Phillip said I could have all the pastries I wanted, so I kept eating. My mother objected and tried to take the tray away. Phillip said we were guests and he would complain to the boss if she refused to serve us, so I had the double thrill of stuffing myself with pastries and seeing my mother unable to stop me.

My mother's birthday was December 1st; I wanted to have something special for her, but there was nothing to get. I usually wrote her a poem and made a little card, but it never was something that really pleased me. This time, I decided to think about what to make early in the year. The acacia tree in the courtyard was still blooming and I wondered if I could make perfume out of the blossoms, perhaps adding some of the jasmine. It seemed like a great idea. I remembered that, before the war, I saw Aunt Cesia make a lemon drink by leaving a lot of lemon peels in a big jar covered with alcohol. So I collected lots of blossoms and sneaked some vodka from a bottle that belonged to Jasio. I mixed it together and closed it all in a glass jar. I thought it might need a few months to develop into perfume.

In a week or so, the blossoms looked brown and wilted. I thought I should leave it longer and I did not want to open the jar so as not to let the fragrance escape. But as time went by, the mess inside the jar looked worse and worse, and when I finally opened it there was no flower smell, just a smell of rotten food. It was a big disappointment and it made me mad. I decided to go to the big market and, having had a few zlotys put aside, buy real perfume. It was a somewhat scary undertaking; it meant going quite a way across town, secretly at some hour when my mother was working and would not be looking for me.

The "small ghetto," where we lived, was a series of streets that were incorporated into the areas assigned to Jews. Before the war, it had been a middle-class mixed residential area. At the time of the formation of the ghetto, many non-Jews were obliged to move out, which created some available housing. That is why Aunt Cesia was still in her prewar apartment, which happened to be included in that section. Most commercial activity took place in the "large ghetto" that enclosed the Jewish section of town, which had been poor and crowded, full of little shops and artisan workshops, easy to isolate. The two sections were separated by a large avenue, a central city artery for buses and trolleys. To cross from one section of the ghetto to the other, one had to go over a bridge that overlooked the avenue, climbing up a set of stairs and then down, all securely wired closed. I had been there a couple of times with my mother. Not wanting to go alone, I had asked my friend Marek to go with me. It was to be an adventure, but instead it was very frightening.

I remember it as a surreal experience. The market was a teeming crowd of poor, half-starved people, rushing in pursuit of food, buyers, sellers, all looking for what they might need for their immediate survival. Below us, where I was afraid to glance too long, was a normal city. Well-dressed people going to and fro in their usual pursuits. I remember a difference in color. As if in a movie, the ghetto area was in black and white. Below the bridge, there was a little market with fruit and colorful flowers. It seemed to me that colors had begun to disappear from the ghetto. In fact, the following spring, none of the trees flowered any more. I always wondered about that and thought perhaps it had to do with frequent fires and smoke in the air. My memory of traversing that bridge is very visceral. It was like looking down from purgatory into paradise. The life below seemed totally unreal. No one from below looked up and no one above dared to linger and look down for too long. Among the gray market crowd—makeshift tables covered with old clothes, household objects, and occasional food items—small children pushed through the crowd ready to grab at anything that could be had, making all the others hold tight to their purses or purchases.

Later that year, when I would no longer have gone alone, and when the streets in both ghettos were lined with small children begging in Yiddish, I went with my mother looking for bread. We bought a small narrow loaf. We were walking back when a small boy, perhaps five years old, darted from the wall of a building at us and bit into the loaf of bread my mother was carrying. He did not try to grab it, just bit into it. Genia let the loaf go and we quickly walked away.

But at that earlier time when I was there with Marek, I was determined to find what I came for. Sure enough, there was someone selling perfume. I had a little bottle I had brought with me and I looked for my mother's favorite, Chanel No. 5. It was there, but when I handed over the money it turned out to be only enough to cover about one quarter of the small perfume bottle. I took it home. The smell was pretty strong. I thought it would stand being somewhat diluted. So I carefully added a bit of water. To my horror, the whole thing turned cloudy and seemed to lose its fragrance. I remember my disappointment, but I no longer remember what I did with the bottle. I don't think I ever gave it to my mother or remember what I gave her instead. I was too embarrassed at my failure.

All this happened during what I think of now as the first stage of the ghetto, from when the area was first delineated that was to be the Jewish ghetto, in November of 1940, through the time when the area was quickly and seemingly unexpectedly enclosed by a tall brick wall, until the first massive deportation, "selection for resettlement," as it was called, "resettlement in the east," in July of 1942. In that first year, most people still believed that they were merely being interned, as is common in any war. That the internment, though marked by deprivation, would be only temporary, a new "normal" to be managed. It was this belief that made it possible to try to make life as comfortable as possible, with cafés, with friendships, stretching the food, guarding possessions, calming nerves to make them last for the duration of the war, hopefully short. With that in mind, Genia did all she could to convince her parents to come to the relative safety of Warsaw.

Wloclawek, where my grandparents Dziadzius and Babusia lived, was officially annexed into Germany and considered a part of the German Reich. Warsaw, on the other hand, was set up as a "self-governed" area. This allowed greater freedom to Poles as well as Jews. The pretense of self-government made it possible for the German plans of total annihilation of the Jewish population to proceed in a slower, more organized manner, which weakened resistance, giving a glimmer of hope at every turn of events. Each stage of deprivation could be managed, as everyone waited for the war to be over.

In the Reich, Jews had to wear a yellow star on their back and walk off the sidewalk. There were frequent executions and humiliations. It was clear that the Jewish population would not last long. Yet my grandfather resisted the idea of moving to Warsaw. In Wloclawek, he had his own house and his factory. He wrote to my mother that, as a business owner, he would not be treated like the other Jews. His factory was operating; the Germans wanted the product. He had been made the manager; he was indispensable and therefore safe.

She did not believe him. She decided that what was keeping them there were all their possessions, silver, linens, carpets. Once these were transferred to Warsaw, they would be able to come quickly, should they need to leave Wloclawek. Somehow, as she always did, she managed to get all the necessary permits and make arrangements. Sometime later, large cases of packaged house goods began to arrive. I remember the cases standing in the courtyard, as we had no room to unpack them. How long they stood there and when they disappeared I don't remember. Soon there were ordinances that required Jews to hand in all their silver, fur, linens, all objects of value, to the Gestapo. I don't know now whether my grandparents were no longer alive by the time all those cases shipped from them disappeared.

It came about that for a brief time in the ghetto we received food packages from Brazil. These were arranged by Mietek, whose travels, as the map of Europe kept changing, took him from Italy to France, where he was briefly interned by the Vichy French at Casablanca, but managed to escape. He arranged passage on a ship going to South America, stayed for a while in Brazil, then made a hazardous trip back to England on a ship bringing food supplies and braving the German blockade. All this information came by letters forwarded from their friends in Switzerland. As all letters were censored by the Gestapo (did they really read every word?), Genia and Mietek wrote them in a private code. I remember when Genia got one letter she read out loud to Jasio and me: "He writes that he has so much free time on his hands that he is learning to play drums and tying monkeys' tails . . . my God, he must be in Africa!" That was the internment in Casablanca.

And so, when he made it to Brazil, we started to receive exotic items: coffee, tea, canned fruit, and canned fish. Restaurants on the Aryan side gave good prices for such luxuries and that is where Genia decided to sell them. We needed money for daily things like bread and butter and grain or sugar. She wanted to do the dealing herself; perhaps it also gave her a chance to get away. She would go with her friend Phillip on his motorcycle. It was never clear to me and to dubious neighbors who he really was, and why he seemed at liberty to move in and out of the ghetto. Genia treated each trip as an adventure and never expressed any concern about her safety. Jasio, on the other hand, was full of apprehension, of which I was the most obvious recipient. As curfew hour would approach and occasional shots were heard as always from the streets, Jasio would mutter darkly, "One of these days—one of these days she won't come back . . . ."

I tried to fall asleep, listening for her footsteps. She always came back.

Sometime later, when Phillip seemed no longer to be around, she would go by herself. (*Funny, how I don't remember ever asking about what happened to anyone, unless I overheard it being talked about; it seemed that it was better not to know.*) After the war, when someone asked her how she went back and forth from the ghetto, she said that she would take off her armband and mill about one of the gates to the ghetto. The gates had a checkpoint booth with a Jewish policeman on one side, a German in the middle, and a Polish policeman on the other side. It was a busy place of legitimate and illegitimate business. She claimed that she would try to get close to the outside part and then ask the Polish policeman to be admitted to the ghetto. He would ask if she had a pass and she would say no, but she heard it was possible to go in and buy some cheap goods. He would tell her to go away and she would walk off. The return, she said, was more difficult.

A particularly vivid memory of an exotic package is a can that arrived with no label, and we had no choice but to open it. It was a large, oblong-shaped can that contained pineapple cut into spears. I had never had pineapple before, and that taste and smell of it still stay with me. Later, when food got really scarce and leaving the ghetto more difficult, we ate the tinned sardines. Those cans were often our only meal.

At some time during that first year in the ghetto, some Christian organizations arranged mass baptism for children and others who were willing to undergo conversion. My mother thought that maybe the church would then arrange to try and save the baptized children as Christian souls, and that seemed to have been the promise. At the last minute, she backed off herself. She pushed me forward to have prayers said over me and I was sprinkled with holy water. Our names were collected and I am not sure if some certificate was issued, but it was a small hope of being saved. Later, when passing as a Catholic on the Aryan side, I was always grateful for that ceremony. It saved me from worrying that I was committing the mortal sin of having my first communion, which I had later, and all the other sacraments, while never having been baptized. At the time I would have found that very upsetting.

It seems to me that my mother missed no opportunity to gain an advantage or to have a bit of normalcy in our lives. Maybe that is why it is so hard for me to remember the dark part of that time. For example, she had made me very proud of my long hair. It had never been cut, and fell below my waist. With lack of heat and hot water, she would find a hairdresser in the ghetto where she would take me to have my hair washed and dried once a week.

Aunt Cesia took me once to a children's play (King Macius), which was put on in the famous orphanage run by Janusz Korczak, who had written the play as a children's book. That memory, too, has imprinted itself on my mind. My mother braided my hair and rolled a braid over each ear, fixing it with a large bright ribbon. I was dressed in a freshly ironed dress and went with my aunt, who was wearing a big brimmed hat. Cesia was very active in the ghetto as a doctor and provided services to the orphanage, so we had a place of honor in the audience. The orphaned children were dressed in uniforms and the boys' heads were all shaved and the girls' hair cut as short as could be. There was already a typhus epidemic in the ghetto, carried by lice, so the luxury of my long hair, which my mother insisted on and which she carefully combed and checked for lice every day, made me feel really strange.

I will never forget that feeling of alienation. The children all looked thin and sickly, and sad. I thought that I had nothing in common with them. I was sorry I had to see them. I thought they must look on me like some strange nasty creature. I had such mixed feelings of wanting to be one of them, and wanting to make sure that I was different, that my fate was different. I did not know how to feel. I was sorry Aunt Cesia had brought me; I just wanted to go home, away from those sickly, hateful children. The confusion of feeling that I did not want to have anything in common with those children still haunts me. I had to be polite and pretend to my aunt how much I enjoyed the excursion, while terrified the whole time by the fate of the orphaned children.

I recently saw a photo of Korczak's orphanage—the sight brought back all those feelings quite undigested. The orphanage and Korczak's story are quite famous now. When the children were being taken directly to the ovens, as it turns out, Dr. Korczak had them marching down the street singing, as he led the procession. The rumor was that as a famous scientist who had grown up as a Christian, he was told by the Germans that he could go free, but he refused to be parted from the children and kept their spirits up till the end.

That winter and the following spring, the food shortage became more acute and the sense of doom greater. The café was no longer open and my mother would not let me out of her sight. We often went out looking for food to buy or for a charity soup kitchen, several of which had sprung up, run by the *Judenrat*. The mother of my friend Ella was able to get some beets, which she used to bake for us in the stove. We ate them sprinkled with sugar as a great treat.

Jasio began working at the *Umshlagplatz*, the train station from which deportations were taking place. His job was to unload the trains that brought in supplies for the Germans. Thus, he was able to hide different bits of food from what was coming in and bring it back to us. Going out with my mother, I saw groups of people huddled around garbage cans and other refuse looking for food. Like ghosts that would appear one day and be gone the next. They did not speak Polish; they were strange and frightened. They were gypsies and Jews from countries west of Poland, including Germany, "in transit to resettlement in the east." We were told to keep away from them as they might carry infectious diseases, just the way Aryans were told to keep away from Jews, who they were told carried typhus.

A sense of doom began to descend on the ghetto inhabitants. It was no longer possible to believe in survival. When the German Jews arrived, I remember people saying: "If this is what they are doing to their own citizens, what will they do to us?" It was around that time that news began to spread that the trains were not resettling people in the east. Someone marked the cars and discovered them returning in a matter of a few hours. Someone else followed the railroad tracks and found them going to strange places, gas chambers. Some believed this, while others refused to believe such news.

In July of 1942, the orders finally came. All people living in the Warsaw ghetto regardless of age and sex would be resettled in the east. Exceptions would be made only for those who had work papers, showing them working in a capacity that was necessary to the maintenance of the German force in the ghetto. This included Jasio's job of unloading supplies. Families of these workers were to be included in the exceptions. My mother had her prewar passport, which listed her under her maiden name, Lubowski, the same name as her brother Jasio. She registered us as his wife and daughter for the purpose of the "selections."

The first selection took place soon after these orders came out. All those who still lived in the building were told to line up. A Jewish policeman, watched over from a distance by an SS man, checked all papers, simply ordering people right or left. It was soon obvious which line was which. Women with small children with no working family head, the old and infirm, all went into the left line, then to be loaded onto waiting trucks. Around this time of final selections, someone had seen Marek running down the street, caught and loaded into a truck. Thus all my friends were lost.

Waved right, we would head back upstairs, not wanting to see the rest of the process. When it was over, Genia told me that Ella, Muha, and their mother had been taken. She said not to worry, because people were taken to *Umshlagplatz,* where Jasio was working. He had the run of the place and he would be able to get them out. She would send him a message right away to look for them.

I went upstairs feeling a great despair. I had to do something. I decided to pray. After all, I knew all the prayers, having always gone to church with our housekeeper before the war, and now I was baptized. I got down on my knees and said all the prayers I knew over and over, for them, for Jasio to help save them, over and over, till I fell asleep exhausted. I waited for news of them next morning, sure that my prayers would have worked. The look on my mother's face told me differently.

"They were loaded right on to the trains. Usually there are a couple of hours in the waiting room and that is the time he can get people out." I cried and cried. So prayers did not work. I was so sure they would.

I searched for Ella during all the following years. Wherever I was, I kept hoping she had somehow survived. I put up signs with her name at survivor conferences, asking for information. A few years ago, when a complete list of victims became available online, I read that Ella and her sister were murdered a short time after that "selection" at some extermination center closer to Warsaw. I named my daughter after her. As for Marek, there was no way to find out. I never knew his last name.

4. The Ghetto, Last Stages

What happened in the last stages of our existence in the ghetto happened so fast that it is difficult to remember the transitions. It seems to me that no one ever told me anything directly about what was going on. Was it my mother's way of protecting me? More likely it was her notion, shared by adults at that time, that small children were immune from reality, just needed to be protected and to do what they were told. They would not understand, anyway. How could they, when it must have been difficult for adults to understand? So everything I knew and everything I remember was overheard or mutely understood. Certainly, the feeling of urgency increased, and with it, the need not to make trouble and to do what I was told.

There was a short period when we simply stayed as close to our home as possible, venturing out when there was a possibility of finding food, mainly a soup kitchen set up by the *Judenrat*. The streets were dangerous and frightening; the typhus epidemic was increasing. Besides the starving and begging children and adults, there were often dead bodies covered with newspapers or rags lying in the street, which were then picked up in wooden carts and taken away.

As an adult, I thought of these street scenes like vignettes from Victorian or pre-Victorian London where middle-class people walked the streets among the beggars and the cripples, the mothers holding their starving children, averting their eyes and holding back the rim of their skirts or coats. There, class was the divide, but for us it was a necessary defense and our divide was proximity to survival.

Jasio came every day and brought us food, mainly bread, sometimes butter, a piece of sausage or the sweet jam made of beets, which had been part of the food rations, when they were still available, to put on the bread. I remember the bread as very dark and heavy. Often there were strange objects inside, stones or jagged pieces of metal, so one had to be very careful eating it. Was that because of the conditions under which it was made, or was it to add to its weight?

The knowledge that deportation meant death must have been universal at that point. I knew it, but it had no name. If you had asked me what I thought happened to my friends, Ella, her sister, and Marek, when they were "taken," I had an image of them falling into a big black hole never to be seen again. I guess that was as accurate as you could get.

Before the final selection, there came a lull in the deportation. Announcements were made that, if certain numbers of people volunteered daily for "resettlement," the selections would stop and life could resume in a more orderly way. Members of the Jewish police were charged with delivering required numbers as the condition of their own survival.

There was information from the *Judenrat* that those who volunteered for "resettlement" were to pack "food for three days, 15 kilos of personal belongings including all jewelry, gold, money and any other valuables."

It seemed like events in traditional fairy tales in which the monster has to be fed a prescribed number of victims every day as the price of leaving the rest alone. For a while, there was a lull in the chaos of selections. I remember walking down the street with Genia, past the city square where those reporting for "resettlement" were to gather. They were mainly older, well dressed. It seemed to me they all looked like my grandparents, with neat baggage and food bundles. Passers-by would yell at them not to go, and some responded that they had had enough, that whatever happened to them was better than staying in the ghetto. Others simply looked away and said nothing.

I heard that many of these volunteers were parents or families of the Jewish policemen, and by giving their relatives the quota numbers they were required to deliver, they were hoping to save their lives. In the beginning, there were rumors of postcards sent from these volunteers, claiming arrival in some safe place. I don't know how many were deported in this orderly way. I do not want to think of what treatment they received upon arrival.

Those remaining in the ghetto now moved about more freely. My father, whom I don't remember seeing in the ghetto previously, appeared one day to say that he was leaving, going east to try to get to the Russian side of the front lines. He must not have been living in the ghetto. He stayed overnight with us, and shared the bed with me, while Genia made herself a place to sleep on the floor. Because of curfew, friends sometimes stayed overnight with us and we often slept three in a bed, with me in the middle. So I was surprised that this was not the arrangement when Bolek, my father, came. I think now he must have come to say goodbye to us. It was the last time I saw him.

At that time, when it became clear what deportation meant, many of my mother's friends had already found ways to escape from the ghetto. They had friends they could rely on. This was especially true for members of certain professions. Doctors, lawyers, actors, and musicians could rely on their prewar Aryan colleagues to prepare hiding places for them. No small matter, as the penalty for hiding a Jew was death.

Aunt Cesia, Uncle Peter, and their son were offered refuge and could have left the ghetto. They were not only well-respected physicians but they had been members of the Socialist Party before the war and the Esperanto movement. They refused to leave, saying that because of the typhus epidemic they were needed. What happened then was that Cesia did come down with typhus, was nursed back to health by her husband and son, recovered, and was told that in her weakened condition she was no longer useful but would only be a burden. She should leave now and they would come later as planned.

Aunt Cesia survived the war, living with another woman doctor as her housekeeper, newly arrived from the countryside. Her husband and son never came to join her.

There were several reasons, I am sure, why my mother would not consider leaving. Jasio was the main reason. She had promised her parents that she would always take care of him, the favored son, and she meant to keep that promise. The other overriding reason was that she had no money. She had jewelry that she saved, but no cash to buy her way out of the ghetto, to pay someone to keep us, which was the most common way to hide. I also think that her sense of being able to handle each situation as it arose and some indomitable belief in our survival must have transferred to me. And of course, I was there. Some people considered a child a hindrance to their survival and felt trapped because of the child. I really believe that, for Genia, my existence was the reason to make the utmost effort to survive, which she would not have had the energy to expend on her own account.

One of the pieces of jewelry that we had was a thick gold chain that had been in the family, made of 24-carat gold. I always marveled at its wonderful bright yellow color. Early in the ghetto, my mother had it cut into three pieces and gave one to each of us, in case we were ever separated and needed some valuable to help us. She sewed each piece into our heavy clothing. Mine was in the bottom seam of a winter jacket. I don't know what its origin was, perhaps a watch fob; it seemed too heavy to wear as a necklace. Each piece was about six inches. I still have mine; I don't know what happened to the others.

Once it was stolen from me and because its loss was so dramatic, the fact that Genia was able to get it back reflects not only her determination, but shows how in the midst of these haphazard fatalities, the ghetto had an undercurrent of secret connections. Somehow, everyone knew where the people they cared about were, could get a message to them, and kept track of one another. Maybe it was just certain groups that had those connections. Anyway, early in our life in the ghetto, I was on my way to spend a few days at Aunt Cesia's. I had a little suitcase packed, which included my jacket with the gold chain in the hem. It seems we stopped to get something or to wait for someone, set the case down on the curb, and it was instantly gone. This story always fascinated me because one would think that this was an isolated act anyone could have perpetrated. Somehow, Genia knew whom to ask for help. She found out who should be contacted, pleaded for the return of some child's worthless clothes, which her daughter needed. It seems that there was a network of thieves, fences, and sellers—an orderly setup that seems hard to believe. I don't know if she had to pay, but the case was returned in a couple of days at most. As we held our breath and opened it, everything was there, my jacket untouched.

Jasio had joined groups of young people, possibly part of the resistance, later fighting in the ghetto uprising. Somehow, he was able to get the work at the *Umshlagplatz*, which was so useful to us all. I wish that I had had the interest when they were still alive to ask questions and get the details of all these connections. But all I wanted was not to be identified with that whole history, to forget, and so did they. Many of our postwar experiences conspired to create this incomplete closure.

Just after the first deportation, it became known that Adam Czerniakow, the head of the *Judenrat*, had committed suicide. He was considered to be clever in negotiating with the Gestapo and had assumed that with each concession he made on the part of the Jews, he had won some assurances of their survival. The rumors that the trains took people to their death, resisted as they were for a long time, the brief appearance of German Jews in the streets of the Warsaw ghetto, and the suicide of the one trusted negotiator with the Germans finally convinced even the most hopeful of the inevitability of the end for everyone. And indeed, the next stage was an order that closed the "small ghetto" where we lived. Everyone had to leave and survival was only available to those who were actively employed in German enterprises. I think the "large ghetto," more densely populated, was still being slowly evacuated, block by block. I remember having to pack only things I could carry in a knapsack. No more suitcases to be set on the curb. I doubled up on my underwear, took a pillow and a blanket rolled up on top of my knapsack, a cake of soap, a toothbrush, and a towel.

What I remember most clearly is that earlier that month I got some flax seeds. I don't know if they were from a supply we got to eat or who gave them to me. I had a small pot that I filled with dirt and I planted the flax seeds. Since I always had some end product in mind, perhaps I just found out that linen is made from flax. I took care of my planting, watering them every day. I sat the pot on the window sill, the same window outside of which I held my book to read by the dying light, and waited for them to sprout. Finally, they did. Long, spindly stems came up, supporting small buds. On the day before we had to leave, the buds opened into tiny flowers of the most beautiful blue. What I most lamented was that I had to abandon my flowers. I knew there was no question that I could not carry them with me; I did not even ask. I also knew that without me they would soon die.

To this day, I have very ambivalent feelings toward plants. Here is what I do: I rescue dying plants from the store, I set them up happily when they start to revive, and then I feel pressured by having to take care of them and I neglect them, thinking they should now make it on their own, and feeling a certain sense of resigned satisfaction when they are finally beyond saving and have to be discarded. I tell people I have a brown thumb. I have never before connected my strange neglect of plants to mourning the flowering flax. If I had any artistic talent, I think the first thing I would paint would be a watercolor of the little pot of blue flowers on the window sill. I mourn them still, maybe as some mourn a pet.

So with my knapsack, I went with my mother to work in one of the workshops maintained in the ghetto by private German companies, who had their goods made by Jewish slave labor. Again, I have no idea how my mother knew where to go and how to act. The shop we went to was called Toebbens; here, German uniforms were shipped in parts to be stitched. The shop areas were complete with extra floor space. Since most of workers were women, there was a space for children to play while their mothers worked, and small food rations were handed out.

I have since learned that the German directive for those food rations was that they were not to exceed 184 calories a day.

Genia had made up her mind that we were not to be separated, thus she would not let me out of her sight. Before entering the factory and registering there, she registered me as over twelve (working age). She got a pair of high heels for me and put a kerchief over my head to make me look older. I was eight and a half, but very tall for my age, and very thin. I had recently been very sick with bronchitis and coughed a lot.

The workshop consisted of a large industrial building with long tables set with sewing machines. I remember it as very disorderly. There were piles of fabric everywhere, and some people slept right on the floors. Everyone had their own pile of material to sew. I don't believe much real work was done, it was obviously a holding operation to delay deportation and make it more orderly. Men and women sat behind the tables at the machines on haphazard chairs and sewed. These were manual machines, mainly operated by a hand wheel. I don't remember ever doing anything but pretending to be sewing. My mother sat next to me doing much the same. I don't think either of us had ever worked a sewing machine before. The very sham of this work made it clear that it was not something that would last.

My memory is that it did not last very long, maybe no more than a couple of days or a week.

5. The End of Safety

It was morning, a couple of days after we joined the Toebbens workshop. And it happened as I was sitting next to my mother, sewing or acting as if I were, when we heard the rumble of trucks outside and that now so familiar word "*Raus*," usually "*Juden Raus.*" This was different. No one entered the shop, and then someone shouted, "They have come for the children!" People ran to the windows. The children were escorted from their room on the lower level of the workshop and loaded onto the trucks. Women were screaming and trying to get out. The doors had been locked. People started opening the windows and jumping out. Genia held me tight and put her hand over my eyes. I still heard the screaming of both the children and the adults. It did not last very long, and the trucks pulled out.

Everyone was milling about and gathering their personal things. It seemed clear that the trucks would be back very soon for everyone. It must have been clear from the beginning, from the makeshift appearance of the shop, which had been there for a while before, that it had just become a waiting station to deportation. Genia gave me my knapsack, took my hand, and said: "See that tall guy on the right side of the table?" pointing to a young man standing near us, wearing a gray sweater. "Follow him, he knows what to do. Don't lose sight of him."

People were trying to leave the building through the front doors. I kept my eyes on the man my mother had pointed out. He edged towards the other side of the room. I noticed that a few other people were hanging back as well, watching him. Then, abruptly, he walked to the back of the room and opened a small door. The small group followed him quickly; we were right behind. He closed the door behind him and we were at the back of the workshop hall, where a bombed-out brick building closed off a small outdoor space. We all walked quickly around the corner of that brick building, out of sight, and saw a work detail, a group of men collecting and stacking bricks. This was one of the jobs that allowed people to have permits to move about as workers. Called "*Placowki*," these groups of men worked both inside and outside of the ghetto doing heavy manual labor, most often clearing debris and collecting building materials. These groups had the freedom to move about, and as long as they were so identified and stayed together, they were not interrupted in their work by the Gestapo. *Placowki* and German-owned workshops were part of the policy to make the remaining Jews useful, as the males in the Polish work population had been depleted by arrest and deportation to German labor camps and the usual attrition of war.

The building we found ourselves next to had been leveled, except for the basement. A black hole appeared in its side, an opening through what had been a basement window. We all quickly crawled in through that opening, while two of the men from the work detail stayed behind us, pushing to move people quickly. Beyond stretched a large basement with a dirt floor. The space was dark and completely enclosed, apart from the opening we had gone through. Once we were all inside, the two men who were outside bricked in the opening. It all happened very quickly and obviously had been prearranged. Genia must have recognized the man we followed as a member of one of the resistance networks.

Once inside, it was completely dark, and we huddled in corners. We were thirteen people. My mother counted and said it was a lucky number. We started hearing a great commotion outside, people running and screaming, German words of command. The group, which had been quiet and determined before, was overcome by fear. It was palpable and, unfortunately with men, it had the effect of making them urinate, which they felt free to do against the walls of the basement. Dust from the floor below us, mixed with the smell of urine, made breathing difficult. I was just barely over my bronchitis, which had kept me in bed for a week previous to this. I started to cough. My mother tried to move us as far as possible from the urinating men.

The sound of heavy boots, which we had heard walking around the grounds, came nearer and the intensity of fear among the group increased. Then, suddenly, the sound of boots was right above us.

The Germans were in the bombed-out building, walking around right above the basement. The tightness in my chest from fear made me cough more; as much as I tried to control it, it seemed as if I could not breathe. One of the men moved towards us.

"If she coughs, we will have to kill her," he said.

Genia waved him away. "I will take care of it," she said. She put her hand over my mouth and held it firmly there. I could not cough, and soon I felt I could not breathe. I tried breathing through my nose but the dusty, stinking air, which seemed to be getting thicker, did not help. I gave in; I thought I could just stop breathing and die quietly.

I think if it had not been my mother, whom I trusted, who was holding her hand over my mouth, I could not have endured it. I remember a blackness coming over me, I faintly heard an exchange between the man on the work detail and the Germans, then suddenly it was over. The sounds died away. Genia took her hand away, and I took a deep breath. I could not believe I was still there. It was probably the worst moment I remember. Just the memory of it gives me a choking sensation, and closed places like that still scare me.

When the Germans caught up with us again some weeks later, I refused to hide again, but this time it may have saved our lives.

The group, except for the man who led us to the hiding place, stayed together after that. We waited at the empty workshop for a few hours. The places that had just been cleared were considered the safest. Somehow word had gotten to Jasio that we were still there. This was always the case; I am not sure how. I know sometimes Genia would corner a Jewish policeman with a message, or perhaps one of a work crew. Since he worked in the visible and useful space of the *Umshlagplatz*, it seems that he was easy to contact. He knew who had just been caught, because they were all funneled through the railroad station. And he had access to food.

One of the oddities of the ghetto was that the phones worked. Perhaps they were a part of the whole city network not easy to detach, and most probably it was useful to the German occupiers to have this means of communication. Hard to remember now that there were no radios and no cell phones, so land lines, unless they were individually burned out or destroyed, would be reconnected and useable. There was a phone at the Jewish police space at the railroad station as well as a few other offices; that is what my mother used, calling from a few remaining public phones to reach her brother, mainly leaving him a message or setting up a time she'd call.

All I remember is that Jasio came, brought us food, and told us which buildings had just recently been cleared and where we could hide. So our group moved from house to house for a while; I am not sure for how long. It could not have been more than a couple of weeks. The German intention of clearing the ghetto of everyone increased in fury. I remember only two places we stayed. One was an apartment where the windows had been boarded up so no light would show, and the group spread out over a couple of apartments for a few nights. It seems to me there were other people still in a few apartments, who seemed to have been hiding before we came. When we moved, it was often just before curfew hour, at dusk.

It is hard to describe what that was like. We walked along empty city streets, where large buildings only very recently emptied of their frightened residents stood eerily empty, all doors wide open, possessions scattered on floors, stairs, objects seemingly still being selected as people were leaving and knew not what to take with them.

In each case, we moved because Jasio would come and tell us what the next move of the evacuation would be, whether the Germans were coming back to check on a particular house or neighborhood, and direct us to places that had just been cleared.

The last place we stayed in is most vivid in my memory. We walked to a building that stood in what was once a somewhat more elegant section of town. The "small ghetto" had been closed off by then so this was in the much larger part of the ghetto. We entered a massive gray stone apartment house, and walked up to the third floor. Somehow, the distance from the street made us feel safer. We walked through the open door of an apartment next to the stairwell. This is another one of these scenes that I can still reproduce in my mind. There were thick drapes in the windows, old mahogany furniture, and large armchairs and big stuffed couches in the living room. It looked like many of the well-appointed apartments from an earlier era. There was still some food in the pots and pans in the kitchen. But what I will never forget and what disturbingly stayed in my mind is the fact that almost the entire living room floor was snowed over with photographs, covering the oriental carpets. I can still see those black and white squares with their ridged edges spread all over. Bureau drawers were left open and photo albums strewn around. It was obvious that as the residents were leaving they wanted to take with them these important pieces of their lives, a hard decision in the short time they were given. As we sat in the apartment and I was tucked into a corner of one of the sofas, I spent a lot of time staring at these photos. Who were these people? What had happened to them? We scooped some up and put them back in drawers, then gave up and walked over the rest.

I have had a difficult relationship with photos ever since. I don't like to commemorate events with photos—I rarely take any, and I don't like to have pictures taken of me. There has not been a time when I have had to deal with photographs that the vision of these scattered memories, meaningful only to those who were already doomed, did not haunt me.

This rather comfortable apartment was our last hiding place. We were awakened in the middle of the night. It was about 1:30 a.m. but there were sounds of trucks, heavy boots on the stairs and the usual cries of *"Juden Raus, schnell!"* We all assembled in the courtyard outside and formed an orderly throng, six abreast. This time, the trucks only came to transport the soldiers who would escort us on our walk to the *Umshlagplatz* and the trains. There was already a line of people caught down the street where the collection had begun. The small group who came out of our building were to extend it.

As we were reaching the bottom of the stairs, about to go outside, Genia grabbed me.

"There is a closet under the stairs," she said. "We can hide there, don't go out."

It was the first time I did not trust her. She was frightened. I had never seen her like that. I started to feel that I was suffocating, with the memory of the basement. A vision of being shot, like an animal in a cage, took me over. I could not believe what I said with perfect

self-assurance: "You go and hide if you want, I am going outside."
I know that I was perfectly prepared to leave without her. It shocked
her, but she believed me. There was no way of knowing which of us
knew better. So we joined the lines walking down the middle of the
street, flanked on both sides by young German soldiers and Jewish
police. The Gestapo members entered the building to search it for
anyone still remaining, and we heard the shots coming from within.

Once we were walking in the line, Genia regained her poise.
"Don't worry," she said to me. "Jasio is there and he will get us out."

It was rainy, a gray October night. I was glad to be in the open air.
The misty rain gave the whole scene a kind of unreality. These were the
final steps that we had avoided for so long. It was hard to believe but
yet almost a relief. The Germans soldiers escorting us were very young,
eighteen-, nineteen-year-olds who could be spared from the front.
Hitler *Jugend*, trained to follow orders and to consider Jews as not really
human, but with no real convictions of their own. There was a clear
sense that they too were caught up in the war and could still be reached
as individuals. The group being led away now already had survived
beyond their own expectations. A bargaining went on. I heard the
woman in front of us offer her diamond ring to a young soldier at our
side, and he turned away with tired irritation.

"I have so many diamond rings I don't know what to do with
them."

In thinking of that scene I have been trying to remember what
language people spoke to each other. I don't really know. I think it was
mainly German, which most people understood. Some sign language
and perhaps even Yiddish.

*Years later, when I was travelling in Czechoslovakia, I overheard a
group of Germans asking some questions and I answered without thinking,
suddenly realizing that I understood every word, though I have always told
myself I did not know any German.*

Perhaps the exchange about the diamond rings was something my
mother told me later. Genia had a very small charming watch, German-
made, which had been a present from my father. She took it off her
wrist and showed it to the guard.

"Oh, that I would take," he said. "My girlfriend will really like it." He took it and we walked on.

Genia was confused. "What can I do now?" she asked.

He looked disgusted. "You want me to take you by the hand?"

As the whole procession turned a corner, nearing the railroad station, my mother grabbed me hard by my hand and pulled me running into a dark side street. We heard shots behind us.

"It's all right," she said. "He took the bribe, he is not aiming at us."

I suppose that was true. I suppose as dead bodies we would be more trouble than as escapees with no place to go. We'd be caught sooner or later.

It was still night, curfew time. Just walking down the street we could be shot. The first thing that Genia did was to take off her Star of David armband and stuff it in her purse. I did not have to wear one, not under twelve years old. I wore one only when we worked at Toebbens to confirm my adulthood. We walked for a few more deserted blocks. It started to rain harder and we looked for an overhang where we could shelter from the rain. There was a large commercial-looking building, fronting a delivery yard. We had just entered into the yard when we heard a set of heavy footsteps, a patrol. A Polish policeman accompanied by two German soldiers.

I started to run towards the interior of the building, but Genia stopped me, and as I stood shivering in the doorway, she marched right out towards the patrol. In a loud voice with a countryside vernacular and accent that was quite distinguishable from occupants of Warsaw, she began to harangue the policeman.

The gist of what she said was: "Am I glad to see you, you got to get me out of here, I am not used to the city, but I was told there was good trading here, and I could buy some stuff and sell it and make some money, so I brought my child with me and I had no idea it would be like that, shooting all over and rain and now that I got in I can't get out. You got to help me to get out of here."

They seemed amused and irritated. I am sure it helped that my mother was a young, attractive woman. "Look lady, we can't help you, we are just looking for a bicycle, we need a bicycle. Do you know where we can get one?"

"How should I know?" she answered in the same tone. "All I want is to get out of here."

"We can't help you, you have not seen a bicycle around?"

"No, how would I know? Just get me out of here." She kept repeating in a whining voice her story of being stuck and wet, and cold and disappointed. They shrugged her off with irritation and walked away.

I stood frozen in the doorway through this whole exchange. I don't think I could have moved. She walked back to me, glowing with success. "Done," she said. "You were so white I was just worried you would faint. I was also worried that they would ask for documents and if I had to open my purse, the armband was right on top."

We moved back on the street as soon as it was past curfew hour. At five a.m. my mother cornered the first Jewish policemen she saw and asked him to get a message to Jasio that we were all right and she would call him. When she finally reached him, they arranged to meet and they hugged and cried as if they had not seen each other for years.

"That's it," my mother said, "we can't wait any longer, we are going to leave today."

It took weeks, if not months, to set up transfers to the Aryan side. She had no money and she had no plan.

6. Jasio's Story and Leaving the Ghetto

The story that Jasio told of that last deportation has defined him for me for the rest of his life and is a gist of what he meant to me.

Jasio had heard that the place we were staying in was to be raided, evacuated, cleared, or whatever it was called. There was no time to warn us. He thought, as Genia did, that he would get us out of the train station, having helped many people that way. He could move about the waiting rooms and platforms freely, could go in and out back doors, and he knew the schedules, routines, and hiding places. But when the transport arrived that morning, he found to his horror that the train was waiting and people were being loaded directly onto the cars. There would be no waiting time, no chance to whisk anyone away. He made up his mind to go with us. He packed a bag, as one was supposed to do for transport, and some food. There was always the hope that the train would arrive at some place where survival was still possible.

He watched as the deportees were being led to the tracks, until he recognized the group we had lived with over these last weeks. He stood by, suitcase in hand, ready to board the train with us. The people he knew gestured to him that we were not there. They seemed quite adamant that he should go away. He was confused; he thought about what to do. He decided it was Genia's doing: she must have known that he would want to join her, and hid somewhere in the crowd—she did this to save him. He decided that he would wait until everyone had boarded and then he would get on and search the train. Surely, he could find us on the train and we would go together. It was while he was standing there waiting that one of the workers reached him to tell him that he had a phone call from his sister.

After that tearful meeting with Jasio, we sat down on the curb and ate the bread he had brought us. Genia repeated that she had had enough and we were leaving that same day. There was no place for us to go either in the ghetto or outside; at least she felt that our luck of survival inside had been used up. Jasio was still safe; he was convinced that he had the job that entitled him to be in the ghetto as long as there was a German in that part of the city. We carried as little with us as possible. It was a chilly October and I doubled up on all my clothes. I did not have much and insisted on taking only my one tiny doll that had no clothes and could fit in the palm of my hand.

When the ghetto was surrounded by a wall, there were a large number of gates for the passage of people and goods, and there was a guard house at each point of entry. Usually, there would be a German inside the guard house, a Jewish policeman on the ghetto side, and a Polish (blue) policeman on the Aryan side. That day, we walked from gate to gate asking questions, running into people Genia knew, trying to find a way out. At almost every gate this was possible, but it required money; the bribe had to be divided three ways and there had to be enough so that each party was satisfied. How they divided it, I don't know, but it seemed it was standard practice. Genia had only jewelry. In the course of the day, we met people she knew who told her that it was possible to cross at the Court building. This was a large municipal building that spread over a whole block, with an entrance on each side of the ghetto wall. I believe that business was still conducted there by both Poles and Jews, so it was not unusual to see people entering there from both sides. She was told that while the doors on the ghetto side were usually locked, there was a watchman who could be bribed to lead people through after closing hours. He was the only one that needed to be paid and the diamond and emerald ring my mother had been saving would do.

So, on the afternoon of the day we had been apprehended, we stood with a small group of people in the vicinity of the municipal building and waited for the appointed hour. After about 5:30 p.m., the door opened and everyone entered quickly (there were six people in the group), when an elderly, pleasant-looking man with the typical long Polish moustache locked the door behind us and gestured to us to follow him. He approached each person and was given the bribe that was prepared. He glanced at each, nodded, and dropped the items in his jacket pocket.

We found ourselves in an imposing building with tall ceilings and mahogany woodwork. We walked through some corridors till we came to a wide marble staircase, which we climbed. All had to be done quickly and quietly, every sound echoing in the empty halls. When we got to the top of the stairs, probably a couple of flights, we went down again to reach the other side of the building.

I felt awkward and scared. My shoes refused to be quiet on the marble stairs, and it seemed that the very beating of my heart reverberated through the building. We were hungry and we had had no sleep. I reached into my pocket where I thought I might have saved a cube of sugar that I could slip into my mouth, but as I searched around, a cake of soap slipped out of my pocket and went bouncing down the stairs, step by step, the sound reverberating, it seemed to me, through the whole building. Everyone froze. Would I again threaten everyone with discovery, as my coughing had done in the basement hideout? A wave of terror and guilt went through me—how clumsy—and there was nothing I could do to stop it. The cake of soap came to rest at the bottom of the stairs, and there was no other sound. We continued. I did not dare glance at anyone. We came to a small door, and the concierge let people out slowly, one or two at a time, which would look to anyone passing by like the normal traffic of late litigants. We were the last ones. I think he knew that we did not really have a place to go. We were uncertain and scared. We might have been entering a foreign country. He walked with us for a few blocks till we seemed a little more steady. He told us how much the bus fare was, which my mother did not know. He wished us luck.

Genia went back to her peasant persona. She knew we looked strange and therefore suspicious. She told me to keep looking around and make loud excited comments about how I had never seen such tall buildings and how exciting it was to be in the city. We looked like strangers and we should act like strangers, hiding in plain sight. Her broad country accent came back and she did not try to blend. It was already getting close to evening curfew time. She had told me that we were going to the house of the only person she knew how to find, Aunt Bronia. This was an aunt of my stepfather, Mietek. She had married a Christian some years before, had converted and lived with her husband where no one knew that she was Jewish. They had an apartment in Warsaw and no children. She did not know, of course, that we were coming, not even that we were alive.

I should mention that the previous October a directive had gone out that any Jews found outside the ghetto without proper documentation were subject to the death penalty. The same applied to any accomplices. A month later, this order was extended by the German Governor of the Warsaw District to say that anyone who gave any assistance to a Jew—lodging, food or transportation—was also subject to the death penalty. This was stated as being for the safety of the whole population of Warsaw "as Jews were responsible for the spread of diseases."

It was under these circumstances that, half an hour before curfew time, we knocked on the door of my stepfather's aunt. I think if she had known who it was she would not have opened the door. She had the most horrified look on her face. She kept saying: "How can you do this to me? We could all die because of you, you can't stay here, you must leave." I don't remember if her husband was there or how he acted. Genia was firm. She walked in and it was clear that she was not going to leave.

"We need some food," she said, "and we are going to stay the night. In the morning, we will leave as soon as the curfew allows. But tonight we are staying here."

I remember that evening well. Aunt Bronia made us crawl along the floor so we could not be seen through the windows, we even ate crouching on the floor. We whispered so neighbors could not hear. She was quite terrified.

As an interesting aside, after the war Mietek sent her money monthly and that is what she lived on. I never knew what my mother told him about that time, and of course she could not be blamed. When he and I visited Poland after my mother died, we went to see that aunt, who was quite old then. I was sullen and quiet. Mietek kept asking me what was the matter.

Wasn't I happy to be visiting? If there was a problem I should tell him. Given the way he was, I did not know if he was ever told and was just trying to goad me or if he really did not know. But later I spoke with another of his relatives, Mila, who had been in Poland all through the war. She was not surprised. "You are not the only one, she turned her own brother away," Mila said. "She would not let him into the house. It was shortly before curfew, he got stopped on the street, and was shot and killed a block from her house."

The next morning, we left early, as Genia had promised. After some consideration about what to do, she remembered that she had a school friend who had an apartment on Zlota Street. It was registered under her own name and no one knew she was Jewish, but then she married a man who was a prominent well-known Jewish attorney, and he had to move into the ghetto. She accompanied him but kept the apartment under the care of their old family servant, a woman from the country, who had taken care of her since childhood. My mother had been a frequent visitor in the house since her teenage years and knew them well. We went and sat on a park bench for a while so as not to arrive too early. It was strange to sit in the park like that, green grass, trees covered with leaves, people walking with dogs, like landing on a different planet. Later that morning, we knocked on the door of a third-floor apartment in a large seven-story building. It was a modern building, built shortly before the war by the Bayer (Aspirin) Company. The elderly woman opened the door and recognized my mother immediately.

"Genia, how are you?" She hugged my mother.

My mother said, "I have to ask you if we can stay here, we have no place to go."

"Of course you can stay here, I am in the apartment all alone. I don't know when the owners are coming. I am keeping it for them. But there is plenty of room."

That was the end of our wanderings, at least for a while.

7. Times of High Anxiety

T imes of high anxiety are etched in my mind in great detail, such as our leaving the ghetto, escaping from the round-up at Toebbens, and the march to the *Umshlagplatz*. But the time afterwards, when things settled down and there was a period of normalcy, I remember very vaguely. And yet the danger was always present and always in the forefront of every day.

The apartment on Marszalkowska Street, which we moved into immediately after leaving the ghetto, consisted of a living room, two bedrooms, bath, and kitchen. At the time we arrived, one of the bedrooms was occupied by a tenant, a young man who was a member of the resistance. My mother turned to him for help, as our main need right away was for identification documents, without which it was dangerous even to walk down the street. The underground, AK (Polish, *Armja Krajowa*), was expert at producing these for a price. We did not have money to pay for the documents, so Genia had to make up a story about why she needed them, without giving away the real reason. She told him that her husband, Mietek, was an escaped prisoner of war and the Gestapo were looking for her, thus she needed to change her name. There was some truth in that. Mietek, who ended his journey west living in France, by that time under German occupation, had been arrested by the Vichy French and was imprisoned in Casablanca, from where he escaped. She chose a name, Krolikowska, typically Polish but close enough to her real newly married name, Krol, hoping that if someone recognized her from prewar connections and saw the name, they might think they had confused her with someone else. She promptly wrote to Mietek through their friends in Switzerland that Mrs. Krol had died and in her place her employers hired a Mrs. Krolikowska, who had a little daughter named Krystyna, and she provided our new address.

Genia's participation in their activities was a favor to a Polish patriot, thus Genia became a working member of the underground, doing small chores such as delivering resistance-published newspapers and messages. Shortly after our arrival in the apartment, the old house-keeper returned to her home village. My mother's friend, who owned the apartment, was making arrangements to leave the ghetto and would arrive soon. In the meantime, the tenant began to bring over men whose identities were no longer safe in Warsaw, who were in transit to partisan groups in the woods and needed a temporary place to stay. The usual routine was that such people would require a disguise, new hair color or beard or a mustache newly grown, at which time a photo of their new face would be taken and documents would be produced with their new identity. This would allow them to board a train to wherever they could be integrated into a fighting unit. Train travel was especially dangerous, as trains were often stopped for document checks and the passengers were trapped, with little chance of escape.

It became my mother's task, one which she did not seem to mind, to take care of these transient fighters. She was an attractive young woman; they were adventurous, brave men. They all had to think that their days might be numbered. I know there was one special person with whom a romance blossomed. It was perhaps at that time that Genia decided to find another place for me to stay. She told me that she was worried that it was too dangerous for me to stay in the apartment and it would be better if I were somewhere else. When I think of it now, it seems that I never questioned her decisions—she had saved our lives so many times and always seemed to know what to do. My task was to make as little trouble as possible. During the time of hiding, I had heard many stories of families whose identity was betrayed by some indiscretion or misspoken sentence by the accompanying child. I was well aware of the importance of my ability not to give us away.

So it was a very traumatic experience when, having achieved a feeling of safety in our new lodgings, and feeling lonely and cooped up in the house, I spoke with a next-door neighbor and offered to take her dog for a walk. I can still remember the pleasure of taking the dog outside, walking around the courtyard with "my" dog, as if I were a normal child with a normal life. Before the war, we had always had a dog. My grandparents had a dog I loved to play with, and

I always liked being with an animal. In my moment of exuberance, I took the dog off the leash and let him run around, taking pleasure in his freedom.

A Polish policeman came by and told me that it was against the law to have a dog off the leash. I was contrite and ready to leave, but he insisted on accompanying me upstairs "to talk to my parents." And so we went upstairs. I worried about Genia's reaction to seeing me come up to the door accompanied by a policeman. I rushed in before she could react, telling her what had happened, acting very upset as if I were concerned about being punished for taking the dog off the leash. This made the policeman conciliatory, telling her that it was not so terrible, he just wanted to give a warning that it should not happen again, which she assured him it would not. I don't know if that incident added to her sense that I should leave. Being cooped up in the apartment with no company and perhaps crimping her lifestyle seemed like a bad idea.

Shortly after this, she found a place for me through the AK. In keeping with her story that my father was a prisoner of war, there was no mention of escape this time. It seemed there was a shelter, boarding school, or whatever one might call it, for children of prisoners of war whose families could not take care of them. It was located in a small town outside of Warsaw, and was supported as a charity by Germans and some Polish contributions.

We went by train. My sparse wardrobe packed, I was delivered into a group of rather sullen, hostile children and a few somber caretakers/ teachers. Later, when I read stories by Dickens of such places, these settings were very familiar to me. The children were from poor working-class or peasant Polish families who had no extended family willing to take care of them. The food was to be provided by the occupiers, mainly discarded German army provisions that rotted in transport. There was a constant smell of spoiled food in the air, and when we had the treat of a meat dish, the meat always had a green tinge. Local people provided the school with some vegetables and grains. The children were always hungry, and fought among themselves for any leftovers. There was corporal punishment administered with what seemed to me like glee by one particular caretaker, who carried with her a belt for that purpose.

I started off on a bad footing. The girls' dorm room had a row of cots and a row of cubicles along the wall for outer clothing. The rest was kept in suitcases under the cots. After Genia introduced me to the teachers and said goodbye, I deposited my belongings next to a small cot, one of a row of beds that had been pointed out to me. I had to go to the toilet, and seeing something that looked like the likely door, I went in. It was a boys' toilet. Realizing my mistake, I ran out into the main hall to a chorus of jeering children making fun of me. To get away, I brushed past a large girl who took immediate offense and attacked me. Other children formed a ring around us, ready for amusement. My adversary jumped on me and grabbed my hair. It took me a moment to realize that she was actually trying to inflict pain on me. I was completely amazed. I could imagine sparring, but I could not understand that someone wanted to hurt me. In my amazement, I simply tried to defend myself. I tried to be mean but simply could not bring myself to have the desire to hurt. This has stayed with me. I have never been able to gather enough anger to want to hurt someone physically. It is still something that baffles me.

Somehow, shortly into this skirmish, one of the boys, seeing me frozen in a kind of confusion, came to my aid and pushed my assailant away. He was one of the older boys, who seemed to have the respect of other children. From that time on, he became my friend and protector. While most children seemed to enjoy noisy play, we would go off by ourselves to walk or talk. Once we came upon a group of boys throwing stones at a sick-looking cat sitting on top of a wooden fence. It upset me and I tried to make them stop, but they only laughed at me. After a small altercation, my friend was able to chase them away, and I took the cat back with me. I set up a place for it outside and tried to nurse it back to health, but it died a day later.

I was a very serious child. I think my seriousness and composure set me apart from the other children and confused the adults taking care of us, who were used to intimidating their charges. I was not one of the oldest, but as I was tall for my age I seemed older. When I first arrived, it was soon discovered that my hair was teeming with lice, not an unusual occurrence among the newly arriving children. There must have been other children so infected, but they had short hair and the lice could be combed out. I had long hair that had never been cut, reaching almost to my waist. It was my mother's pride and joy. She would not cut my hair, which I wore in braids rolled up over my ears and held together with ribbon. The immediate reaction to the lice in my hair was that my hair would need to be cut. I said no, that could not happen.

I remember how strongly I felt about it, not for myself, but wishing to preserve the effort that Genia had put into my hair. I simply said, "No, you cannot cut my hair." I was amazed at the sense of power I experienced. It was clear to me that I trusted in my power to say "No." And that if I really meant it, it would be clear to the adults that it could not be done. It was, in fact, clear to them.

When they finally relented, they said, "If you won't let us cut your hair, we will have to pour hot gasoline over it and you will have to comb out the lice and nits, and everyone will watch." I was sat in a chair outside in the yard as hot gasoline was poured on my head and cleaned my hair. Groups of children gathered around me, calling me names and making fun of my infested hair.

As I sat there in some pain when the gasoline scalded my scalp (I was picking scabs of scalded skin for some days after), I remember the feeling of triumph that I can call up to this day, looking at the jeering children around me. "What dummies," I thought. "Don't they realize that I could not care less what they are saying? I have triumphed here, I saved my hair, which is all I cared about, and no one can do things to me I don't want done." I realized then that with enough determination one could say "No" to adults and they would have a difficult time over-coming that. This was really different from the feelings of fear and helplessness I had lived under for so long.

A couple of months after I entered this institution, it was deter-mined that, being ten years old, I should have my first communion. As the arrangements were being made, I was glad that Genia had had me baptized in the ghetto by the hopeful Catholic missionaries. I don't know if they really thought they might save lives, or were just saving souls. But I was spared the discomfort of accepting a sacrament in church which, I was aware, would have been a major sin had I not been baptized. I have a photo of myself in the white dress Genia had made for me for the occasion, flowers in my hair, my long, flowing hair that was my personal triumph.

Genia took the train once every week to visit me. For a treat, she would bring me an egg. If she was able to get it from a farmer on the way, the egg was raw and she would bring a bit of sugar with it. I would beat it up in a dish with the sugar till it became syrupy and eat it with a spoon, very, very slowly. This concoction was called "*kogel mogel.*" If the egg was purchased ahead of time and had to wait for when she was coming, it would be hard-boiled and I would cut it into little pieces and savor each one.

In addition to being tall for my age, I was very thin. The doctor who came to examine the children categorized me as pretubercular; it was determined that a small group of us needed extra food. Some residents of the town had agreed to feed this group of children once a week with leftovers from their table. It was humiliating to go up to wealthy-looking houses, a band of barefoot ragged children waiting for handouts. I especially remember one such instance, when the lady of the house came out, saying to the cook, "Don't let them into the house and for heaven's sake keep an eye on them, you don't know what they might steal." The leftovers that day were tomatoes baked and stuffed with a mushroom mixture. As hungry as I was, I thought they were disgusting and dropped my portion under the porch, hoping some animals or birds would eat it. I have never gotten over my dislike of stuffed tomatoes. They must have wanted to get rid of them too, or they would have just given us bread, which we would have much preferred.

The children all were assigned daily chores: bed-making, cleaning, washing dishes, laundry, and taking care of rabbits that were raised on the property, though I had no idea what was done with them. The chores were posted on a list with the names of children next to them, so that the assignments went in rotation. If one did not wish to do a particular chore, it was possible to switch with someone else on the list. Unbelievable as it seemed to me, none of the other children liked taking care of the rabbits. It involved cleaning out their cages and collecting greens for them, all considered dirty work. So I was able to make this my main chore, and actually gained some popularity for taking the rabbit chore for myself and switching with whoever's turn it was. The cages were set up a little way from the house and I could disappear outside for hours at a time, taking care of the rabbits, alone and quiet.

The other least desirable chore was scrubbing pots, which was my other choice. I got out of doing anything else. That too was done alone, after all the other cleanup was finished, so I was often left alone in the kitchen and liked the looks of the shiny pot. Often, my boyfriend and protector would come to join me and we could talk without being teased by the others.

It was while I was there that I first discovered I was near-sighted. During lessons in class, I knew that, in order to see what the teacher wrote on the board, I had to sit in the first row. I never wondered why; it was just something peculiar to me. I was also the best student in class and the best reader. One day, someone came to test our eyesight. They put a big chart on the wall. "Read the first letter." I did. "Next letter." I could not see the next letter. Impossible, they said, she is pretending. How could she not see this huge letter? I couldn't. Getting glasses was not possible, and anyway, since I had managed this far, after a while it was ignored. I just had to go up close to things.

In the winter, one of the chores we had was to walk in the woods and collect firewood for the kitchen stove. When it got cold, many of the children resisted going outside; malnutrition makes one susceptible to frostbite. They would collect their coats, hats, and gloves, stuff them under the bed and hide there themselves, while the caretakers checked the rooms to make sure everyone was out. I actually liked collecting firewood. It was useful, it made it possible to walk through the woods, and it was an escape from supervision, as long as you brought in armfuls of dry twigs for the fire.

One day, something else happened that I never really understood. We were told to go and play outside, not told to collect firewood but just to play outside to get fresh air. Everyone was to leave the building. It was very cold, and there was some attempt to hide inside, but eventually I think everyone left. Actually, I did not do much with the other children and I certainly did not know how to play. I don't think I have ever learned how to play to this day, even as I raised my own children. So I thought it would make sense to collect firewood and went off to do this. When I returned with an armful of wood I was confronted with a very angry adult, the mean one.

"Who told you to collect wood?" she stormed. "You were told to go outside and play." I was doubly shocked, since I expected to be praised for my diligence.

"You will have to be punished," she said and marched me to the bedroom. "You are to sit down and write a letter to your mother telling her what a disobedient girl you have been, and how disappointed we are with you."

I thought it was the most ridiculous and incomprehensible demand. There was no way I would do such a thing. I looked at the woman in amazement.

"No, I am not going to do that," I said. "My mother has more important things to think about." It was the second time since I had been there that I felt the certain power of "No."

"All right, if you'd rather be whipped," she said, "that's up to you." She pushed me down on the bed and began to get the belt ready. I don't know if she expected me to cry or object, but I remembered the power of staying calm.

"Ok," I said, "if that will satisfy you."

She looked a little shocked. "How many times?" she asked.

I thought for a moment of what might seem reasonable to her, so I would not make her more angry, without too much pain for me. Three seemed reasonable. "Three times," I said. She had knocked me over onto the bed, on my belly, so I could not see her. Then I heard the door open and close, and waited. After a minute, I realized that she was gone. I got up and that was the end of it. I was never hit in that institution and never threatened again. The other children began to notice and made annoyed comments about my privileged status. "How come you never punish her?"

I never told Genia anything about what went on there; I did not want her to know. When she asked, I always said that everything was fine. Years later, she heard me talking about how the children were beaten and mistreated, and she got very indignant.

"It is not true," she said. "You never told me anything like that. I would have known if that was going on."

The following summer, several of the children, myself included, came down with scarlet fever. We were placed in isolation in a darkened room for the duration of the illness. When the symptoms of scarlet fever subsided, I was still ill. As a complication of scarlet fever, I came down with rheumatic fever and was sent to a clinic in Warsaw. The treatment, as I remember, was large doses of salicylic acid, an awful-tasting substance, and "cupping": glass cups heated to create a vacuum and placed on your back to draw out the "bad" blood. Sometimes, the resulting cupped flesh would be cut with a razor to increase the bleeding. At least I was again in Warsaw and my mother could come to see me.

I don't know how long I was sick, and I have no lasting effects from that illness. But at the time, weakened by the illness, I did not return to the institution. Instead, I went back to live with my mother to recuperate. Things had changed a lot in the Warsaw apartment. The tenant was long gone, as were his activities. When my mother's friend, the owner of the apartment, finally was able to escape from the ghetto, she came with her husband and her mother-in-law. Jasio, as I already knew, had arrived the previous February, two months before the ghetto Uprising. He came out through the sewers. After having been sure that his survival was certain and his identification, which he wore as a number on his chest, made him safe, he was walking down a deserted ghetto street with two other workers, also identified by their metal numbers, when they came upon a drunk German patrol who, for no apparent reason, just for sport, decided to scare them by shooting at them. The men tried to show that they were legitimate, allowed workers. Exactly what happened was never quite clear to me, as Jasio did not like to talk about it. His two companions were shot dead, one on each side of him. He dropped on his knees and started to plead for his life. The Germans waved him off, laughing. He walked away and made immediate arrangements to get out of the ghetto. He escaped one night through the series of sewers that were maintained by the organized

Jewish resistance fighters in the ghetto preparing to fight the Germans, in conjunction with the Polish underground, who helped to provide them with arms. He was lucky in that he had a place to go, to his sister's.

The tenant was asked to leave, as there was a concern that his activities—the fact that he kept guns and resistance newspapers—were endangering all the people there. His response was that, since they were all under a death sentence, it did not matter what contraband was found with them. In the end, it was the sheer number of people in the apartment that probably made him leave. At one point, my mother's friend wanted her and Jasio to leave also, but at that time a decree came out that there had to be a certain number of people registered per apartment or a tenant would be assigned. Since only the owner of the apartment, my mother, and I had documentation, our presence saved the apartment from being made available to strangers.

The apartment now contained six Jewish refugees. As I read other stories of people hidden in Warsaw, it seems a very rare situation that a normal apartment, not a hiding place, was totally under the control of its Jewish occupants. There was no one to bribe, no one to be beholden to or to be afraid of. But the utmost care was required to maintain this and preserve the look of normalcy to the casual observer. The owner of the apartment, Ana Makowska, had always been registered as an Aryan. She passed as a non-Jew, kept her apartment under her real name, and only moved into the ghetto to be with her husband, a well-known Jewish attorney. His looks would have betrayed him on the Aryan side. Accompanying them out of the ghetto was his mother, an elderly Jewish woman who spoke mainly Yiddish, and could not be seen or (especially) heard. Ana herself had spent much of her childhood in Germany, where she was educated, and she spoke fluent German. She had an older brother who had been living in Germany, was married to a German woman, and had a child living in Berlin. While no one knew he was a Jew, he was known for his anti-Hitler political activities; at the beginning of the Nazi regime, he was interned in a concentration camp for political dissidents. Ana corresponded with her sister-in-law and was very concerned about the child, little Maria. Sometime later, Maria's mother was also arrested and friends of the family arranged for the child to be brought to Poland to her aunt. She was a charming little girl, who looked a lot like Shirley Temple; many little girls were dressed like that at the time. I think her guardians arranged for her to be sent to Poland with some German army personnel.

When I came back from the clinic to live with my mother, six-year-old Maria was there as well. Ana had realized that having the child in Poland would not guarantee her survival, and was looking desperately to find her a home back in Germany.

While Ana's husband and mother-in-law never left the apartment, and were not supposed to be seen by anyone, it was a bit different with Jasio. He was a handsome young man in his late twenties, not disposed to stay hidden patiently. His coming and going could not happen completely unseen, since there was a vigilant concierge, common in all European apartment houses, whose business and legal responsibility it was to know who lived where, and a lot more. To make it possible for Jasio to be occasionally seen leaving the house, obviously having stayed the night, Genia let drop some discreet hints that he was her lover and maybe sneaked into the house late at night. The concierge enjoyed being a party and a co-conspirator to this dalliance.

For Jasio, who had been an active and rebellious youth, and who then went through the harrowing ghetto experiences but did his utmost while we were all still in the ghetto together to help and feed us, the enforced inactivity of hiding was like torture. In April, two months after his escape from the ghetto, the handful of people remaining there fought the Germans and were annihilated. The entire area was burned to the ground; the fires were visible from far away. It must have been hard for him to see and to know what had just happened to all those whose fate he had shared for so long. Two months after that, in June, there were rumors of a possible miraculous reprieve. It is now known as the "affair Hotel Polski."

A Jewish organization, the Relief Committee of the World Jewish Congress in Switzerland, had arranged for passports and visas, and in some cases offers of citizenship in Latin American countries.

It was explained, by rumor again, that the Germans, having destroyed the ghetto and with it the remaining Jewish population, realized that whoever was now surviving in Warsaw was well situated and not easily to be found. Attempts to identify Jews one by one seemed inefficient. For those who knew of such hiding places, blackmail was more profitable than turning people over to the authorities for certain death. It was also assumed that those who had survived had the means, the money, to maintain themselves. Since their lives would be saved anyway, so the argument went, the authorities could provide them with safe passage out of the country, possibly exchanging them for German prisoners of war in other places. So notices were posted that if such individuals would give themselves up and bring a large sum of money, they would be housed in a specially reserved space, Hotel Polski, in Warsaw and then sent out of Poland.

Though the notices were at first viewed with suspicion, a few individuals who could no longer handle this hidden existence arrived at the hotel. Huge sums were asked, which somehow seemed to people to lend credibility to the scheme. Soon, news came that letters from the Hotel Polski refugees were now coming from Cyprus and other places, telling of their good fortune. Those who arrived at Hotel Polski with money were well treated, given legitimate-seeming documents and promised a speedy departure. Later, history determined that, while the exit visas and transport were paid for by families abroad who thought they were saving their relatives, many of those whose names were provided had long before perished. The Germans simply changed the names on the documents and collected the funds.

At the time, Jasio wanted nothing more than to join the Hotel Polski group. As a man, his life was always in danger through easy recognition. In Poland, only Jews were circumcised; when a male's identity was questioned, this kind of "inspection" made any pretense impossible. It was a special danger for hidden families with male children.

I was not there at the time, but I was very aware of the tension and divisiveness of this plan. I knew that Genia was very mistrustful of the whole setup. The idea of willingly giving oneself up into the hands of the Germans, after all the effort to escape, was quite unthinkable to her. But Jasio was despondent and adamant. There was no question of all of us going. He was willing to go by himself. Maybe in the end that separation would have kept him from joining in, but as it was, it couldn't happen anyway. The sum of money demanded was well beyond anything they could afford. Genia made a half-hearted attempt to raise some money, but it was not possible.

This feverish hope lasted maybe a month. Soon, there were other rumors: of no news from the deportees, of the fact that maybe the happy reports were just forced messages written on the way to the gas chambers and then posted from exotic places. Soon, Jasio accepted the idea that, by not having the necessary funds, he had probably escaped certain death.

I looked up the data on Hotel Polski recently because it had been such a strange and sad matter for us. It seems that, of about 3,500 people who gave themselves away, only one or two hundred survived.

So, in a way, though we all lived together, each family was in an intense struggle for survival, focusing on their own problems. Ana's attention focused on her family's survival and the fate of her niece Maria. All shared the problem of financial survival.

I don't know how the idea came about for making pastries. But that was the activity they settled on. Genia would buy supplies on the black market—flour, butter, whatever other ingredients were needed. I assume that, since her employer bought bales of cotton thread this way, there were available contacts. Such foodstuff was only available on small individual rations. Jasio and the others who were secret inhabitants of the apartment baked at night. The shades were down then, as they needed to be since the time of air raids, so no one could be seen. During the day, the baking crew slept and was not around.

The only problem with this set-up was the use of cooking gas. The excessive meter readings would have aroused suspicion. To prevent that, the gas meter was disconnected every night and by-passed. One of the by-monthly crises of this existence was the anticipation of the meter reader's arrival. It was necessary to make sure that the meter was properly connected, that there were no signs of any activity that could make him suspect that the meter had been tampered with. His arrival was not regular enough to be easily anticipated, creating constant anxiety.

There was a hiding place that an architect friend of Ana's designed to fit those who were not to be seen inside the apartment: Jasio, Ana's husband, and her mother in law. What had been a walk-in pantry off the kitchen was now walled off, with a shallow, moveable shelf. The open space in back was just enough to squeeze in these three people. (This may have been a common kitchen design in new modern apartments. I was amazed when, not too long ago, I saw a photo of a similar arrangement, taken after the war by a survivor from Warsaw.)

The decision to hide, prompted by any unwanted visitor, or the monthly arrival of the gas meter reader, was a source of great anxiety. Survival was a continual guessing game. The gas meter reader had no regularly scheduled time, although one usually knew when he was in the building. There was a worry that he would notice some alterations to the mechanism or a lingering smell of gas, which sometimes escaped when the fittings were fiddled with, and finally there was the danger that one of the three hidden individuals would make a noise.

Space in the apartment was limited with all of Ana's family there. My return was not welcome. The bedrooms were occupied and the hidden occupants, who worked at night making pastries, slept much of the day, reducing their visibility. My mother and I slept in the living room with Jasio when he was done with his kitchen work. Our make-shift sleeping setup consisted of the living-room couch extended by three chairs, turned on their side, so that their backs continued the couch. Our heads rested on the couch back and our legs were stretched over the backs of the overturned chairs. The whole surface was covered with a layer of blankets. The chairs were secured to the legs of the couch with rope. It was not very comfortable, but somehow we all slept. The daily setting up and undoing of this cumbersome arrangement was Jasio's job.

In the early evening when I could help out in the kitchen, I would take maraschino cherries out of a jar and hand them to Jasio, who then put each in his mouth and sucked them dry, so no red syrup would run out to mar the little mounds of whipped cream he placed on the pastries. He often said that it pleased him to imagine that some Gestapo officer, now the main clientele of the upscale restaurants where Genia delivered the pastries next morning, was eating his spit. On her way back from her job, Genia would pick up the pastry orders for the next day.

Genia worked in a black-market workshop—one of many cottage industries set up by enterprising individuals who, like us, purchased materials on the black market and sold the goods the same way. This particular workshop belonged to a prewar friend of hers, who was Jewish but married to a Catholic who was an American citizen. Henrik was a child of Polish immigrants who, like many others, emigrated to the United States in the late 1800s. Some years later, they decided to come back to Poland, bringing with them their young son born in the States. Early in the war years, he had privileged status, but was careful to protect his Jewish wife. Later, when America entered the war against Germany, he too went into hiding. Everyone attributed his ingenuity to his "Americanism." He had installed two machines that were set up to make small household-size spools of yarn from large industrial cones. This setup was in a kitchen of the apartment where he and his wife resided. He bought the large spools somewhere illegally and distributed the small ones to eager customers, as everyone wore mended clothes. All his employees were either Jews or a few others hiding from the Germans. According to him, this made the whole operation safe, as no one would give it away. He and his wife did indeed survive the war and eventually came to America. This work and the pastries were a necessary source of income.

Ana and her family were well-to-do; at that time, though, her energy and money were absorbed by trying to ensure the safety of her little niece. Six-year-old Maria was a German citizen, which meant that she had special privileges, better food rations, and her own documents. But soon it became obvious to her aunt that she could not ensure her continued safety in Warsaw. There were no other relatives in Poland, but there were contacts in Germany who were willing to take the little girl, so arrangements were made for her return to Germany. As none of those details were shared, I know little of how it came about. All we knew was that, when arrangements were made for her travel, a high-ranking Gestapo officer who was returning to Germany agreed to escort her there. She was an enchanting little girl, very used to being with strangers, and he was happy to take her with him. She was going to a family friend in Dresden.

On the day he was to arrive, the apartment was all spruced up. Only my mother and I could be seen. Everyone else was in the kitchen hiding place. This visit and the departure of little Maria, accompanied by a Gestapo officer in a freshly pressed uniform, shiny polished boots, greeting us with "Heil Hitler" and giving us a military salute for a goodbye, may be one of the more bizarre memories of my childhood.

The story has a very sad ending. While Ana corresponded with the caretakers of her niece, and had many photos and letters, by the end of the war Dresden was one of the most heavily bombed cities in Germany. She lost track of Maria and of the family who took her in. After the war was over, Ana devoted years, money and energy, to look for her niece. She never found her or anyone who could tell her if her niece survived.

One day, as I was coming home from the store, I found the street blocked off, with trucks, soldiers, and police. I was told no one was allowed in. It was our building that was cordoned off. It was the first building from the corner. I tried to edge closer to the front entry and was stopped by a policeman. No one was allowed in, except the residents.

"Do you live in that building?" he asked. I had a moment to consider. Was it us they were after and should I go in? My mother was at work; I knew she was not there, but Jasio was.

"No," I said, "I don't live there," and I walked away.

"They are breaking into a third-floor apartment," I heard someone say. We lived on the third floor, where there were four apartments. Many of the apartments were requisitioned for use by Germans, as it was a nice modern building in one of better sections of town. It was thought that made us very safe, as no one would suspect that we lived in the midst of the enemy.

Ana was allowed to keep her apartment because she had had it for a long time, thus had seniority. When one of us was returning home, we would casually run the key over the wall as we came up the stairs. It would reverberate inside our rooms and was a signal that it was one of us coming up the stairs. Otherwise, one had to be careful not to open the door to the wrong person. Several times, tipsy German neighbors would ring the bell or try to get in with their key, and one had to be careful to send them away without offending them.

I walked off towards my mother's workplace and told her the street was blocked off and the house cordoned off by German trucks. Obviously, they were looking for someone.

By the time she walked back with me, all was clear. It must have been very frightening to those in the apartment. The story we heard from excited bystanders was that a person who apparently was staying in the apartment right next door to us was wanted by the Gestapo. When he realized that they had come for him, he left through a window and slid down a rain pipe. The building backed onto a courtyard where a restaurant on the cross street had its back entrance. He went through the back door of the restaurant and out the front. Anyone who had seen this would gladly cover for him. By the time the gendarmes broke the door to that apartment and realized he had gone out the window, they could not get to the restaurant, which was actually almost a block away on the cross street.

The slightly guilty feeling that I was quite ready to desert the people in the apartment stayed with me. It was the same feeling that I had when, at the end of our ghetto escape, I refused to hide with my mother. Somehow the notion of survival, pure survival, made for very clear—if uncomfortable—choices.

As an adult, I judged friends by whether they would try to save them-selves and then possibly be there to help me. The kind of loyalty that would make one say, "If you are going to die, I will go with you," never seemed desirable or attractive.

After the bout of scarlet fever, followed by rheumatic fever and mild malnutrition, my health was not very good. My mother worried about me and was told by the doctor who treated me that I was anemic and should have an egg a day, a tablespoon of butter, a tablespoon of sugar, and a cup of milk. This prescription was more than she could manage. In a couple of weeks, shortly after little Maria went back to Germany, I came down with terrible stomach pains. Jasio wanted to give me some digestive medicine. Aunt Cesia said to wait, so Genia would not let him give me anything. This time, Cesia did come over as my pains increased. She examined me quickly and said it was appendicitis. Jasio carried me downstairs and they hailed a *drozka*—a horse-drawn carriage (there were no motorized taxis, as all gasoline was only for military use). I remember the pain as the carriage rattled over the cobblestone streets. It was the worst pain I had ever had.

Cesia was waiting for us at the hospital. My appendix had ruptured and I was running a very high fever. After some consultation, the doctors decided I was not a candidate for surgery. I would not make it. As I heard later, no one wanted to do the surgery. They thought my chances of survival were minimal, with spreading infection from the ruptured appendix, and did not want a death on their records. A priest was called and administered last rites, my third sacrament.

In the end, Cesia prevailed on the physician friend in whose house she was living. She would do the surgery as a favor for her friend. An operating room was prepared. I remember the bright circular lights over my head and the nurses (they were all nuns of a nursing order who wore large winged caps that made them look like some kind of angel) preparing me on the operating table. I could hear the voices of the surgery group and I became terrified that they would start operating before the anesthetic took effect. I tried to move and could not; I tried to speak and no sound came out. How could I let them know I was still awake? All I could move was my little finger and I started to wave it desperately. I was later told that, as they started to make the incision, one of the nurses said, "Look, she is moving her finger." They stopped and checked, but I was no longer conscious.

This was all before the widespread use of penicillin. There were no antibiotics. My incision was left open and a drain was inserted to divert the pus. My fever stayed high for a couple of nights, and I was delirious. I remember the delirium and the pain. There was a terrible noise in my head and I thought airplanes were landing on my bed. I was furious about it and kept asking my mother to stop the airplanes from landing on my bed. She stayed all night by my side, perhaps for more than one night. She feared, as she told me later, that in my delirium

I would say something that would give us away. But I just complained about those noisy airplanes.

The news of the turn in the war was bringing new hope. The allies were winning. Germany was retreating, but slowly. It now became a matter of surviving until it was over. The allied armies were marching towards Italy, but very slowly. The current joke was that the Allies must be very pious—they were going to Rome on their knees.

Bulletins from contraband short-wave radios were passed around. A Polish government-in-exile had formed in London and was in contact with the Polish resistance, AK, the conservative arm of the under-ground. At same time, elements of the resistance who were left-wing, the socialists who were much decimated by German persecution, many having been known for their prewar activities and hunted down, looked to the Soviet Union as the most likely liberator. Most Poles, however, did not want to repeat the history of Russian dominance that held Poland captive for several generations.

News of the war's progress and the political divisions were almost all the adults talked about. Food was getting more scarce. It seems that all the meals I remember were composed of rice (why did we have rice in Poland?), a heavy, dark bread that was part of food rations, and thick, rough-textured jam, made of beets. When I fussed and refused to eat it, Genia would say to me very good-naturedly, "Just pretend it is something else, something you like, like cake." She knew I had a sweet tooth. She seemed to find her suggestion very funny, which abso-lutely infuriated me in my helpless frustration. It seemed an insult to swallow this horrible fare telling myself that it was cake or meat and potatoes. Even potatoes were hard to come by and the meat that was available as a rare treat was horsemeat. Most of Poland's agricultural products were now requisitioned for the German armed forces; very little was available to the Polish population. When it came from the countryside it would be smuggled at much personal risk to the smug-glers and a commensurate expense to the buyers.

Once, having made friends with a young boy whose feet were wrapped in newspaper, as he had outgrown his shoes, we realized that my lace-up boots that no longer fit me were just his size. Somehow, he

73

had a jar of bacon fat that he was willing to trade for them. What a triumph! I was so proud of being able to bring that jar of bacon fat to our house. It created all kinds of delicacies, like fried onions on fried bread. I think the fat itself was such a treat. I remember eating raw oatmeal, which seemed very delicious to me. I also discovered that chewing on candles made a very satisfactory snack.

The news from the front, fervently repeated and sought from those who might have had access, however dangerous, to shortwave radios or foreign press, made it seem as if the end of German power was imminent. This made the resistance movement more daring and the authorities more vigilant. Assassinations of German authority figures, touted as punishment by the underground press, resulted in roundups of random members of the public, to be sentenced to street executions. The ratio of ten Poles for one German kept being increased, to fifty, a hundred, in an attempt to frighten the population into turning against the resistance activities. The roundups of able-bodied individuals, from trains, streetcars, or wherever they could be found, to be sent to Germany to work in war-related production, increased as Germany was suffering defeat.

The Russian armies were advancing from the east. The type of German occupying forces was changing. The elite Nazi Gestapo officers were less frequently seen and there were more ordinary German army personnel, the *Wehrmacht*. These were not the elite fighting forces, who were now sent to more important places, nor the political stars, who might have gone back to Germany, nor the Hitler *Jugend* trained to hate and hunt Jews. They were just ordinary Germans conscripted to fight in a war that was not going so well now, worried about their families back home. Even as a ten-year-old child, I had a sense of that change.

There were rumors of underground resistance plans to liberate Warsaw, now that the German defenses were weakened and main forces needed on the front lines. Genia, who had still maintained her contacts with members of the resistance, was wary about this event. Jasio could not wait. It was clear that, due to the proximity of the eastern front, Poland would be liberated by the Russians and, as the

AK feared, beholden to their government. Should the capital be liberated by Poles themselves, however, ahead of the advancing Russian army, and if the Russians were met by representatives of the free city of Warsaw, so the thinking went, Poland could then dictate its own terms of liberation and need not again fall under Russian domination.

The Germans stationed in the city were well aware of the impending danger, so any furtive movements were met with violence. The resistance planners had carefully prepared for the Uprising. It was to happen at the end of the work day on Friday at a time when most people would be at home. Resistance fighters would distribute themselves through the city the night before. Arms were distributed to all those who were to take part. I suppose it was too much discipline to expect from men who had waited now for four years since the defeat of 1939.

That Friday morning, as my mother was on her way to work, a newspaper seller near our house said to her, "If I were you I would stay home today and not go anywhere." She understood and came back. Later that afternoon, there was a skirmish between a German guard and a young man, who, being armed, shot the guard. Others came to their aid, and all of a sudden the whole city erupted, at a most unfortunate time. A great many people were caught away from their homes. All public transportation was halted. Chaos ensued. The German forces brought in large guns and reinforcements from the front lines not far from the perimeters of Warsaw. It was the first of August and the Uprising lasted for two full months, bringing with it a whole new set of dangers, hardships, hopes, and modes of survival. At least we were all together. Had it not been for my health problems, I would have been cut off in another town, with who knows what consequences.

8. August–October 1944: The Warsaw Uprising

Forewarned by the news seller, my mother, who so easily made friends with everyone, stayed home from work and even managed to get us some food supplies. When the first gunfire broke out prematurely, many were not so lucky. Most of the working population were caught on their way home, faced suddenly with halted public transportation, having to dodge gunfire on the streets. Many did not make it back to their homes for days or weeks, and by the time they got there, their families were likely to have been displaced or lost.

The resistance fighters were mostly members of AK, with a small number of leftists (socialist or communist branches of the underground resistance). Many of the latter had already been decimated by the Gestapo or political enemies within. They all now wore long-discarded Polish army uniforms, or red-and-white armbands over their regular clothes, indicating their underground army (AK) membership. I don't know what it was like in other parts of the city, but where we were in the central part of Warsaw, there was immediate liberation. Polish flags were hoisted over the Post Office, the bank, and other official buildings. The war was over, the Germans were gone. German nationals who had lived in our building seemed to have disappeared. Some were forcibly taken away by the AK and set to building barricades. There was general euphoria. People broke out spontaneously into patriotic songs and the Polish national anthem. When we stepped out of the apartment, at least those of us who were not easily identifiable, we were no longer Jews, but patriotic Poles—sincerely so.

It was good to see all the young resistance members, men and women, swarm into the building and along the streets. We were told that many parts of the city were now completely under control of the

Polish fighters. Everyone assumed that the Russians would arrive shortly. How long can it take a winning army to cross a river? It was thought there would be a political advantage, much desired by the provisional Polish government in London, to greet them not as liberators but as guests. There were many prominent Polish nationals accompanying the advancing Russian army. Many were political activists—socialists and communists who had escaped east—knowing they were on the Nazi list of political enemies. At the onset of the war, they had access to cars and money and reasons to leave quickly. Many of these were Jews, ready to form a new liberal government. That was not the plan that western allies had for Poland at the time. A political struggle was already brewing.

But for now, in those first days of August, we were all facing a common enemy—Germans—having endured five years of oppression, fear, and humiliation. Finally, there was open camaraderie and great anticipation of freedom. More than anticipation. In spite of the imminent physical danger, freedom was actually already here. I can still call back that feeling of finally, *finally*, joy. There was still danger, maybe even immediate danger of death. But it turns out that the excitement of freedom is not lack of fear, but the ability to fight on one's own behalf. The difference between being in prison or on the battlefield.

Barricades were immediately built in the streets at all intersections, using available furniture, trams and buses, carriages, and whatever could be found in the streets. Everyone participated. Molotov cocktails were being prepared for street fighting.

There was euphoria, and even those who might have thought that the action was foolhardy on the part of the insurgents would not express such sentiments. The dark note throughout this time was a constant stream of frightened, desperate people coming through, trying simply to get closer to their homes and families. Bystanders would offer them food or help and they would move on. What it meant to us was that no one was looking for strangers any more—we were all Poles united in our hatred for the German occupier and our support of the insurgency. It would never occur to us to disclose the truth about who we were, but maintaining the Aryan identity seemed no longer to be a burden.

77

To watch the brave young people with their red-and-white insignia gave hope to all. It seemed as if the war was indeed over.

It took the Germans only a day or so to turn their long-range guns towards Warsaw. The patriotic foolishness of hanging Polish flags from liberated buildings was soon clear, when these buildings became primary targets. There was not much air bombardment; perhaps it was too close to the Russian front and their anti-air artillery. The main weapons used were long-range guns, the Big Berthas. They were strangely frightening weapons. You would hear a noise that was a lot like a loud cow mooing, and then you knew that a missile would hit its target in about ten seconds. But of course you had no way of knowing what the target was. There was not enough time to hide, barely enough time to hold your breath.

The building we lived in had a basement two stories deep that had been used as a storage facility by a furniture company. It was a natural shelter. The underground made it their headquarters. Part of the basement was set up as a field hospital, with nurses and a few doctors. Medical supplies were needed. House residents contributed their linens and other material to be cut up for bandages. Those treated in the "field hospital" had mainly bullet and shrapnel wounds. Used to sporadic lack of electricity throughout the war, everyone had carbide lamps, which gave off a very strong light. For some reason, the central part of Warsaw was not heavily assaulted at first. We heard that there was heavy strafing and missile attacks on other parts of the city.

Though I was not allowed to go outside of the building complex, I could be out in the courtyard where trash and discarded objects were accumulating. I wanted to help and somehow got the idea that by boiling cloth I might be able to make cotton for the nurses to use. There were a few other kids around, and I talked them into this scheme. We gathered broken pieces of wood, made a rock fireplace, got a large iron pot somewhere and proceeded to boil water into which we threw strips of assorted fabric. I was very excited, thinking that, if this boiled down to soft cotton for covering wounds, we would be heroes. I never got the chance to completely test my experiment. We were scolded by concerned adults for starting a fire in the first place and ridiculed for what we were trying to do. I was never fully convinced that, given a chance, we might not have succeeded.

The building itself was five stories high. We lived on the third floor, and so felt relatively safe from air attack. Most residents of the top floor had moved their main living quarters to the basement, and the space became divided into little corners with a bed or chairs or any furniture that could be of use claimed by the various apartment tenants. We often spent nights there and the days back in our apartment or milling about the building. It was a typical European apartment building of the time, which meant that there was a heavy door that closed off the entrance from the street. It led into a wide corridor that opened onto an enclosed courtyard. Two staircases leading to the different parts of the building opened from the corridor. In the front was the concierge's apartment with a large glass window in the door that she could open to deal with passers-by, collect rents, or check documents. It was her job, usually the wife of the couple, janitor and concierge, to know everything that was going on. When the building was closed, which was most of the time, it created a lot of space for use.

As food became scarcer, there would be forays to search for supplies. A nearby granary was hit by a mortar shell and caught on fire. People from surrounding residences converged on the building, put out the fire and collected some of the supplies. Jasio and Genia went. Our big score was bags of dried peas, which for some time became our main meals, very versatile. My mother brought back bags of burnt barley, which she would then brew, which made a reasonable coffee substitute. It seemed that the Germans had limited resources and concentrated their assault on other parts of the city. But moving about was not easy. There was news one day that the AK had opened a soup kitchen a few blocks away. Genia said we should go, just the two of us, and get some food. We walked just one block, staying close to the walls of buildings for shelter, when we heard gunfire, stopped, and ducked down. This kept repeating, and so dodging, stopping, crouching in a doorway, an hour had passed and we still did not reach the soup kitchen, which was four city blocks away. The strafing got more intense and Genia decided to turn back. The whole fruitless trip took us two hours and I don't know how we could have carried anything back.

We lived day by day, because the expectation was that this could not last more than a week, then two weeks, then maybe a month. How could the Germans be held off? Why had the Russian army, only a few miles away, not crossed the Vistula River? But the major expectation, perhaps fostered by the AK with its London connections, was of help from the allies. This was the expectation, shared by many, that there would be allied paratroopers parachuted into the city to help the insurgents. So our eyes were always on the skies, waiting for that help.

In fact, the allied forces did attempt to parachute food supplies. So when the chutes appeared in the skies, everyone thought that this was it, help was coming. But the food delivery was not very successful. The way the city was divided between insurgents and the German army, it was difficult to predict if the supplies would get into the right hands. The packages, bags of flour or sugar, would break on landing. The effort was soon abandoned. The paratroopers never came.

But, one night, a plane delivered an emissary from the west. I have often tried to find out in historical texts who it was and how it was described. I have never been able to find any information, but I was there and I saw him. He had an unfortunate and somewhat embarrassing accident. When his parachute came down, he landed on an outside balcony of our building. These were iron balconies with decorative or perhaps protective spikes along the railing. One of these spikes speared his buttock and he was placed in a secluded section of the field hospital for recovery. Important AK people came to speak with him, but he never went outside and in the end, presumably after he recovered, he was whisked away. Flown back to England, is what we heard. It made the possibility of help arriving even more real. But it never happened.

As the insurgency entered its second month, hope for victory, for the arrival of the Russian armies, or for any delivery of help from the West began to fade. The food situation became desperate. I saw a man in the courtyard defiantly skinning a dog and preparing to roast it, while its woman owner cried. This must have been a common occurrence;

doubtless, there were no dogs or cats left. As the population began to sink into a sense of defeat after the initial euphoria, there came an announcement from the Germans, in the form of leaflets and loud-speakers from German-occupied parts of the city, that they understood that there were many civilians who did not sympathize with the insurgency and so should not suffer unnecessarily. So, the announcement said, there would be a cease-fire the following day from noon till four p.m., and anyone who wished to leave the city would be allowed to do so if they appeared on the street carrying a white flag.

On noon of that day, small groups of people began to gather outside, some carrying their possessions or pushing prams with small children. They were few and they were harassed by the bystanders. An elderly woman, seemingly hysterical, was leading them, yelling for everyone to join, to save themselves. She had had enough; she did not want to fight any more. The heavy door that led from the building to the street stayed wide open, once the shelling stopped, and people were gathered at the edge of the street, ready to retreat at a moment's notice.

Jasio, excited by his new freedom of being able to move about and talk to people, was very intrigued.

"Don't go outside," Genia said.

"But they are not shooting."

"Don't trust them," she insisted, and she would not let me cross the entrance beyond the gate onto the street. Jasio could not resist the spectacle of the hysterical woman.

As he stepped fully out into the street, there was a burst of shell fire, and he fell back against the building. A shell had exploded against the wall of the building across the street and a piece of shrapnel lodged in his upper thigh. Someone came up with a stretcher and he was carried into the basement hospital. He was not badly wounded. Once the bleeding was stopped, it was not practical to remove the metal shard, which was in quite deep. It was just a matter of letting it heal over and making sure there was no infection. For that, he had to lie still and try not to move till the shrapnel was properly healed in. The new concern was the young pretty nurse who was attending to him. Would she notice that he was circumcised, would that be a problem?

I don't know how that went exactly. I know she was attractive and he was a flirt. Was he simply able to be very modest or was she charmed or did she not care? But nothing adverse happened. It took about a week or ten days till he was healed enough to be able to walk and join us.

That was one of my mother's long-lasting *I told you so*'s. But, as often happened, it may have saved our lives in the long run. Not long after this false cease-fire, the assault turned onto the city center. We were told that the Germans had left the sections on the other side of the city still in the hands of the insurgents and had begun a fierce bombardment of the city center where we were. The underground moved their headquarters, a passage was created through the sewers, and slowly those who had been sheltering in our building began to move out. First, the members of the underground, then all those who could take their few possessions and make their way to the other part of the city. Slowly, the freedom fighters had to give up block by block. There was no way we could move. Jasio was not well enough to walk or crawl those distances. It was out of the question, so we did not even think about attempting the transfer, but awaited our fate.

Years after the war, I met an American pilot who was stationed behind Russian lines to deliver food to Warsaw. He told me that it was an impossible task. Not only did they not have any way to target the deliveries properly, they could not fly low enough to ensure the safety of the supplies. Flying any lower or more slowly would have exposed them to anti-aircraft guns. It was a very strange experience, talking to someone who was actually there, in the sky over Warsaw at the time.

The news from those who drifted into the building was that we were surrounded. Only a few city blocks with ours in the center remained under control of the insurgents. There would not be much time left before we would be overrun. All residents would probably be told to leave the building and then shot; there was nothing else to do with them. The greatest fear was that the German forces fighting in the city, which were hard to spare from the front lines, were a selection of misfits and, worst of all, Ukrainians: known for their cruelty, who had fought alongside the Germans on the eastern front. Their hatred of Jews as well as Poles had long historical roots.

It was during the newly concentrated assault on the central section of the city that our apartment building was hit directly. We were spending most of our time in the basement shelter, but once in a while we went upstairs to get something or to see daylight. I was in the bedroom that afternoon and Genia was in the bathroom when I heard the "mooing" of the Big Bertha louder than I had ever heard it before. There were only seconds until the hit. I wanted to run but it made more sense just to huddle in a corner. There was a loud shock, the building shook and right in the middle of that sunny afternoon, everything went black. I did not know exactly where I was. Was it safe to step outside the room? I called out to my mother and heard her calling me. I stepped out of the bedroom, walking gingerly in case the floor was not there. We met half way between the rooms and held tight to each other. Gradually, the darkness cleared. It was dust that was settling down. Amazing how the brick dust made for complete darkness. The top two floors above us were pretty much gone. Our third-floor apartment was now the top floor. I don't remember there being any casualties—maybe some people slightly injured by fallen debris. Everyone must have been downstairs.

We rushed back to the shelter. Running with us was a small dog that was on fire. It was a very frightening sight and most people seemed worried that he would set other things ablaze. I ran through the nearest open door and grabbed a blanket, which I threw over the dog. Its owner appeared and took over.

From that time on, we did not venture much upstairs except to get any leftover food. A neighbor whom we had only known in passing had been a tenant in the apartment above us. She had no place to go and asked if she could stay with us. This was somewhat disconcerting, given who our group was, but it was impossible to refuse. She also had something to hide. It turned out that she had been sheltering her dog, a very small terrier that had just given birth to six puppies. It also appeared that she had a great deal of cash on hand and was thus able to purchase food for her dog and pay off would-be attackers. She was very frightened and wanted to have people she could "belong" with. The adults conferred. It would cause suspicion to refuse her, she was only one middle-aged woman, and she had money, which none of the rest of the adults had, and was willing to spend it in exchange for refuge. So Pani Marta became one of the family. She was told that Ana's mother-in-law was deaf and dumb and not to try to communicate with her, and that Ana's husband had been slightly injured earlier, which accounted for a bandage across his face that covered his unmistakably Semitic nose. I was, of course, delighted to have access to the puppies.

The shelling of the house was the last attack we experienced. Almost immediately afterwards, the areas of attack shifted back to the other side of Warsaw. Perhaps there was intelligence that the insurgency fighting forces had escaped there earlier. The German forces receded and our "free area" expanded. Those who had left earlier began to struggle back. But this was difficult, as the routes were now known and canals were destroyed and areas shelled. Only a fraction of those who moved out were able to come back. Some thought it was provident of us not to have left, but I think we would have gone, or Jasio would have insisted on it, following the underground leadership, had he been able to move.

It was becoming sadly clear that the Russian front would not move, that the western allies were not able or willing to offer any help to the insurgency, and that neither the underground fighters nor the civilian population could hold out much longer. There was news on short-wave radios of allied victories and progress, but none of it seemed to bring the end of the war any closer to us. The Russians stopped across the river and stayed there. Some athletic young people dared to swim across to bring news of Warsaw's situation. One of them was a young Jewish woman, the eighteen-year-old niece of a friend of the family. She returned to the city with the advancing Russian army with the rank of a lieutenant and a medal for her bravery.

Although the Germans were not easily able to deploy their fighting forces away from the two fronts to fight this city struggle, to the Poles it looked as if the bravery, the loss of life, and the hopes of liberation were all for nothing.

The fighters numbered altogether about 42,000, of whom half were killed in action. Including civilians, the number of deaths is variously

estimated between 150,000 and 250,000, possibly half the population of
the insurgent areas and a quarter of the overall Polish population of Warsaw.

Now, the question was how to end this struggle without a blood-
bath for the insurgents or the populace. Once again, the headquarters
of the AK underground were in our area. There were rumors that the
insurgents were negotiating with the German authorities for an end to
the hostilities. The conditions, which we were told the Germans had
accepted, were that the underground fighters would be treated as prisoners of war under the Geneva Convention. There would be no reprisals
against the civilian population and food would immediately be brought
in to the city.

The date was set for October 3rd. The last night of the Uprising
will remain with me for all time as one of my most moving memories.
We still did not venture far so my images are limited to our block of
buildings. It must be remembered that we were in a situation that not
many were able to share. Throughout the entire Uprising, from the first
to the last day, we were never in German hands. Two months of war,
but relative freedom, an illusion of having overcome the occupation.
It is hard to describe the palpable tension of the insurgents. They
fought, they survived, they mourned their dead; but they were going to
end with honor, very important to a Polish patriot.

There are elaborate army procedures for retreat and cease-fires. All
were adhered to. The underground members gathered in the streets
singing patriotic songs. Believing that they would be treated as prisoners of war according to military Geneva Convention rules, couples
who had fought side by side made sure that they would be recognized
as being of equal rank. Uniforms were exchanged. Insignias were
designed and sewn on.

They mourned their fallen comrades, but they believed that their
defeat was honorable. In all the writings about the Warsaw Uprising
that I have read, I have not heard this night described. It made a great
impression on me. By midnight, the German soldiers moved in, and to
protect the population, the insurgents remained armed. In front of the
buildings, ours and the ones I could see down the block, there was an
armed insurgent at one side of each building and an armed German

soldier standing a few feet away. Each had his hand on his weapon; neither moved.

In the morning, there was another ceremony. Singing the national anthem, of which the opening lines are, "Poland is not lost yet as long as we are alive," the fighters laid down their arms, formed marching throngs, and left the city, still singing as they marched.

There has always been controversy about how far they got, how they were mowed down. Was it Germans or Russians who killed them? Maybe I never really wanted to know.

Later that day, trucks carrying water, potatoes, and bread moved through the city, distributing the food. It looked like the pact would be kept. As the food trucks arrived, they distributed flour, potatoes, and the ubiquitous beets. Potatoes were the food I most missed. They used to be a part of every meal. I never imagined that one could so crave potatoes. It must have been what everyone else wanted also, because by the time we had our turn at the distribution truck, all the potatoes were gone.

That afternoon, I noticed that someone had dumped a pile of potato peels into a garbage bin standing outside. I scooped them up, carefully separating them from other refuse, and carried them upstairs to cook. I thought the adults would be as pleased as they were when I brought the jar of bacon fat. But to my surprise, Genia was horrified.

"No," she said, taking the armful of peels from me and throwing them into a garbage pail. "We have not sunk so low yet. We will not eat other people's potato peels."

I was disappointed about the potatoes and hurt by the disapproval.

This respite following the end of the Uprising did not last long. In spite of the supposed agreement of no reprisals towards the civilian population of Warsaw, the food trucks were followed by trucks with loudspeakers advising people that the city was to be evacuated. Each section of town would be assigned a time by which everyone had to be removed. Once people were informed of their evacuation time, they would have four hours to empty their homes. After the specified time, the building would be burned to the ground with flame throwers and anyone still found would be killed.

The evacuees were to gather at certain collection places. For us, it was the central railroad station, from which people would be sent to work camps in Germany after a medical evaluation. So we were back where we started. No way could the two men go through a medical exam. Nor did any of us want to be separated or sent to Germany.

We chose a few belongings to take with us and began to wander around the city, looking for a way out, other than the central railroad station. We were now two males, two women, and a child, with our neighbor pushing a baby carriage containing a nursing dog and six puppies.

9. Leaving Warsaw

We had left our apartment, taking with us whatever seemed reasonable to carry. A small suitcase, a knapsack, and for some reason I always had a pillow. The city itself, which we really had not seen for two months, was a terrible sight. I have seen photos of it since and when I see them, it is as if someone suddenly presented me with a recurring nightmare that I barely remember.

Most buildings were severely damaged. Rubble was everywhere, often gathered into abandoned barricades. Overturned tramcars and all other large objects had been piled everywhere as temporary barriers. Here and there, there were still uncollected dead bodies, simply moved to the side and covered with newspapers, and bone remains of horses that had been slaughtered for meat early in the fighting.

Among this debris, throngs of people were wandering along the streets, some looking for family members they could not reach during the fighting and who, if still alive, had moved on. Others, dazed perhaps from being hidden somewhere for all that time, were just confused about what to do. Still others, for lack of another direction, were heading to the central train transfer station. I know we had only one purpose, to find a way to leave the city without going through the German checkpoints. That should have been possible, given a large, familiar city. But as the areas around the city were emptied, there were patrols everywhere, and one could be seen only going in one direction, to the railroad station. Our false documents, hard-won and intended to identify us as not being Jewish, were now suddenly useless. They identified us as residents of Warsaw, a useful identification a while ago and now one that made it illegal to be found outside the city limits. It almost seemed that it no longer mattered that we were Jewish. We could now be shot as residents of Warsaw who did not obey the evacuation orders.

But one thing was really different. The uniformed Germans enforcing these orders were not the smartly dressed SS officers we were used to seeing. They were field soldiers, members of the *Wehrmacht*, looking as confused and tired of war as some of the milling population. They wandered around in twos and threes staring at the destruction around them, thinking perhaps that this is what their home cities might look like now. It still amazes me how quickly people around perceived that difference. It was almost as if these soldiers were not the enemy, but people like everyone else caught up in this awful slaughter. It seemed clear that were they to identify someone as a Jew, they probably would not care.

Jasio must have been aware of that as well. He was wandering around, looking for possibilities. Just then, Pani Marta, our attached neighbor, came looking for us to say that she had located a person with a wagon who could possibly be paid to take us out of the city. He was a *Volksdeutch*. These were Poles of German descent who had the opportunity at the beginning of the war to declare themselves as German nationals. This entitled them to better food rations and other privileges. Such a declaration was very controversial. The German authorities insisted on it if they were aware of the proper documentation. Those who refused, not wanting to be identified with the Nazi ideology or because they wanted to be considered Poles, were often persecuted and punished by the Germans for denying their nationality. They were seen as political enemies of the German Reich. Those who accepted the categorization were looked at as enemies by their Polish neighbors. There must have been some individuals who used that categorization to make themselves useful to the insurgents or their neighbors, but I had always been used to viewing declared *Volksdeutche* with great suspicion. Anyhow, here was a man from outside Warsaw who had come with a horse and wagon to take his family out of the city. He had a pass for four people who could leave with him. He could not find anyone he was looking for. The house was no longer standing. No one knew what had become of its inhabitants. He seemed quite amenable to selling the places on his wagon. By the time we got there, Pani Marta had already struck some kind of bargain and he was impressed by her cash. Still, he was nervous about taking more people than the number listed on his pass and with different names that might or might not be checked.

He had seen on his trip into Warsaw that the city was circled with checkpoints, and he was concerned about being stopped.

Pani Marta was already on the wagon with dog and puppies. The plan was that Ana's mother-in-law, her presumably injured husband, and I would get on the wagon. The rest of the adults—Genia, Jasio and Ana—would follow on foot. The driver was not reassured; in order to prevent him from reneging on the arrangements, it was decided (I don't know whose idea it was) that all would be fine if we had a German escort out of the city.

Jasio at that point was feeling, perhaps, a certain camaraderie with the German soldiers. They were his age and seemed to be wandering about somewhat aimlessly, or perhaps he had a surge of energy from being out of the constant state of hiding and fear. Anyway, he took a camera he had saved and packed, and with his smattering of German approached some of the *Wehrmacht* soldiers who did not seem to be doing much, to ask if they would act as an escort for us out of the city. Maybe they saw it as a lark or a way to get something for themselves in this confusion, or a pleasant assertion of their own interest in disobeying orders, if there were any orders. In any event, two of them agreed. In an hour, they would be off duty and could leave. One took the camera, the other fancied Jasio's watch. We loaded what we had on the wagon and waited for them to appear. They arrived as the driver was getting more and more anxious and we took off.

The horse moved at a slow trot, so that the adults who were walking, as well as the German guards who were now flirting with Ana and Genia, could keep up with us. It was reassuring to be leaving the city and to see them all following us. We got to the checkpoint, a barrier in the road with a guarded booth. The guards looked briefly at the pass, spoke with our escort, and waved us through. As soon as we were out of sight of the checkpoint, perhaps no more than a mile out of the city limits, our escort turned back.

The wagon driver looked around at all of us on the wagon, and at the three adults following behind. I don't know what was going through his mind. He had seen the cash that Pani Marta seemed to be carrying; there were our suitcases on the wagon. Who knows what his intentions were. He suddenly whipped up the horse and took off at a good clip. I saw my mother and the others getting smaller in the distance. They were gesticulating wildly, but I could not hear them. I yelled or maybe pleaded with the driver to slow down, to wait for my mother. But he murmured something about having to go because there would be another checkpoint and he did not have the right papers, and he went on. There was no traffic on the road. I was getting very frightened. The old lady started to whimper; Pani Marta looked confused. At one point, a shiny black SS officers' limousine passed us on the road and slowed down to take a look at us, which was even more frightening.

After about half an hour, we arrived at the second checkpoint. The guard came out of the booth and walked over to the driver. "Didn't you leave some people behind?" he asked. The driver grew pale, being very scared. The guard looked us over and told him to pull off the road and wait there until the other people arrived. The driver was mystified. We all were. How could this checkpoint know about the rest of the people? This was before there were any of the communications so common now. There would have been no way for anyone to get in touch with this outpost or even to know about us.

So we waited. We were all convinced, as the wagon driver must have been, though no one said it out loud, that when the rest of the adults arrived we would all be arrested.

It seemed like forever till I saw the three figures in the distance walking towards us. I waved furiously. When they reached the wagon, the guard came out again and asked: "Are these the people you left behind?" The driver nodded, looking terrified. "OK, you can go now," the guard said and waved him on. The driver was silent and white-faced. As soon as we were out of sight of the checkpoint, he pulled the wagon over and began to throw our things over the side.

"I want you all out," he said. "I am not taking you any further."

We had no idea where we were. Pani Marta tried to negotiate with him for taking us to the next village. He would not hear of it. "I don't know who you people are, I just want you gone." And he drove off, leaving us at the side of the road.

We were all somewhat dazed by what had just happened. We were delighted to have been reunited, frightened by the experience, and those of us who had been on the runaway wagon were completely confused. We moved off the road and made a space for ourselves in the surrounding bushes, out of sight of the road. We were on the outskirts of a village. Here and there, we could see a farmhouse in the distance.

The story emerged of what had happened. As the wagon with me and Ana's family disappeared from view, Ana, Genia, and Jasio tried to run as fast as they could but realized it was hopeless. They were frantic.

Just then, they saw a shiny black German limousine appear down the road, the kind used by high-ranking SS officers. Ana must have made an immediate decision. She jumped out into the path of the car and waved it down. She had to overcome the irritation of its occupants, but she was an attractive young woman and spoke impeccable German, having been educated in Germany. She told the officer in the back that she was a German citizen who had been living in Warsaw and had just made arrangements to leave the city with her friends. The wagon she had hired to take them out of the city had just driven off with all her belongings and her friend's family, leaving them stranded. Herr Commandant just had to help them, perhaps give them a lift.

No, she could not prove her identity as all her papers were on the wagon, but what she could show him were letters addressed to her Warsaw address from Germany about her niece who was living there and about whose welfare she was very worried. She had the letters in her handbag. There was a picture of the beguiling Maria whom she had shipped off to Dresden. Perhaps she even had a last photo of Maria as she was leaving on the train accompanied by an SS officer.

Those letters and her speech were persuasive enough. She was told that, unfortunately, regulations did not permit offering a lift to civilians but that certainly the wagon would be stopped and made to wait for them. This is how it came about that we were dumped at the side of the road by a frightened and angry driver with no idea who we were, but who did not want to proceed with us any farther.

As we sat in the bushes, we could see a short distance away a farmhouse at the outskirts of the village. But who would be there and would it be safe to approach them? After a short deliberation, Genia decided that I should be the one to go and check it out. If there were Germans inside I was just to back out and say I had made a mistake. After all, I was just a little kid; I was looking for a friend or whatever would seem appropriate, and then I should come back with the information. I left my baggage behind and walked over as if I were on a local errand.

I knocked on the door. I think someone answered or it was simply unlocked. I walked into a rather large room, which adjoined a farm kitchen. In the center of the room was a big round table. There was a smell of food cooking. The people around the table, variously dressed, were clearly refugees from Warsaw. In the middle of the table was a large bowl of cooked potatoes that they were all eating. I never knew what actually happened. It was one of those strange moments that, to this day, seems taken out of time and reality. I know that no words were exchanged, but as I stood there staring at the people at the table, a man got up, walked toward me, and handed me his spoon. I moved forward as if hypnotized, sat in his chair, and proceeded to eat the potatoes that were still in his bowl. It was only a few minutes before the door opened and my mother walked in. She had followed me, worried about what I might find, and surprised when I did not reappear quickly. I was terribly embarrassed to have forgotten all about them, and to this day I am amazed at what I must have projected to make this stranger react as he did. Of course, everyone there was a refugee from Warsaw and knew what we had been through. The house was like a way-station where people could spend a night or two, get their bearings, and move on.

Which is what we did.

10. Waiting for the War to End

Within a day or so, a place was found for us at a small neighboring farm. The family consisted of a couple with two sons in their twenties and an elderly grandmother. They grew some potatoes, onions, carrots, beets, and the usual ground crops for their own use. They had one cow, a horse, and a few chickens. Over the house was a large hay loft, which is what they agreed to rent to all of us. We settled in, dividing the loft into separate spaces and arranging the hay into more or less comfortable beds.

The space was hardly room enough for seven people. We paid the farm wife for food that she cooked for us, mainly with money that belonged to Pani Marta, who was less and less happy about being the provider. Ana and her husband and mother-in-law, who had been used throughout their lives to a much more comfortable existence, were busy looking for other lodgings. It must have become clear to Pani Marta by that time that all or some of us were Jews. She was not about to denounce us, but she no longer felt comfortable.

Only my mother attempted to make friends with the farmer family. She always seemed comfortable in any setting. She helped with the cooking and cleaning up the house downstairs, and talked to the elderly grandmother, who slept in an enclave behind the cement chimney of the wood stove in the kitchen. Jasio helped to dig ditches for storing the harvested vegetables and roots for the winter. I helped to line the ditches with layers of straw and filled them with rows of potatoes, carrots, and onions. They were teaching me how to milk the cow. I learned to draw a thin stream of milk and aim at the cat who sat in the barn at milking time, waiting for such a treat.

For breakfast, we would have noodles cooked in milk. The dough was mixed from flour and eggs in a large bowl, then rolled between the palms of whoever was cooking into skinny rolls and dropped into boiling milk. Sometimes pieces of tried out bacon were also floated in the milk. The elderly grandmother made bread right in the wood stove by her sleeping pallet and the house would fill up with the wonderful smell of freshly baked bread, which could be smeared with the bacon fat. I thought it was great, but the rest of our group were not satisfied.

The house consisted of two bedrooms, one occupied by the farmer and his wife, the other by their two sons. The loft with its occupants was not a happy place. We were meant to be in transit. Transit to where? The war was meant to end. But when? Nerves were becoming frayed. Pani Marta was getting more and more concerned that her money would be taken by someone in the group. I don't remember how soon she found a place to go to or whether it was before or shortly after the "diamond ring" incident. That incident was the defining end to the cohesion of our group.

All of us had some hidden jewelry or other valuables for emergency purposes. I had a piece of a heavy gold chain still sewn into the hem of my jacket. Jasio had another piece like it. Ana had a large diamond ring that she wore on her finger, once out of Warsaw.

One morning, she woke up in a panic. Her diamond ring was missing. She was sure it had been on her finger when she went to sleep that night, but it must have slipped off while she slept. It was now lost, like the proverbial "needle in the haystack." She and her husband became quite hysterical. Everyone jumped in to help, but that was the problem, they did not trust anyone to return the ring if they found it. So Ana's husband—who, after all, was an attorney—devised a system in which he and Ana gathered all the straw on their side of the loft and, checking it handful by handful, transferred the checked-out handfuls to the other side of the floor, where the rest of us waited. I don't remember how long it took. It was very tense. I remember it as actually being quite fun. The ring was never found, and by that time the whole setup made no sense.

They were concerned that it might now be evident to the farmers that their tenants had valuables. There was a real sense of antagonism among the group; maybe there was more going on than I understood.

It was October and getting colder. The loft was drafty and not comfortable. Very soon after this incident, Ana and her family left. I started coughing again and Genia was worried about my breathing in the hay and the approaching winter. She conferred with the farming family, and it was somehow decided that Jasio could share the downstairs bedroom with the young men of the house. It was just a matter of putting a mattress on the floor of their room. They clearly liked my mother and wanted us to stay. She could sleep in the kitchen. But I was still a worry.

We moved freely about the village, going to the store, delivering things to neighbors, going to church on Sundays. Still it was fairly obvious that we were city people and did not belong. Once in a while, German patrols went by and checked documents. There were a great number of refugees from Warsaw, and perhaps it would have been more trouble for the Germans stationed there to pick them up than to turn a blind eye. Genia claimed that one time she was walking across a field and was hailed by a passing sentry. She simply ignored him and kept walking. He stared at her for a while, then shrugged his shoulders and turned away.

In the usual way of refugee grapevines, my mother came back one day saying that she had found our Aunt Cesia. She was living in a neighboring town about ten miles away. This meant a lot to my mother. Cesia, her mother's youngest sister, was very close to my mother, who relied on her a great deal. It seemed that Cesia was actually providing medical care to people in her village, something she always did. According to her socialist background, she believed that medical services should be available to all, whether they could pay for them or not. Before the war, she worked mainly in free clinics, saying that her husband's practice was enough to support the family. Now, she was also the only medical provider for a convent and the convent-run school. The original nunnery had been destroyed, and the convent was given the use of a large estate whose owners had escaped the occupation.

In no time at all, I was enrolled in the convent school, for which my mother was to pay a fee, reduced because of Cesia's services. There was no money for it, but Genia did not let that worry her. She promised a payment. My stuff, the little I had, was packed. Somewhere, a winter coat was found along with a knitted hat and mittens, and I was sent off to school. We took a local train there. Cesia met us and introduced us. It was clear that she was well liked and respected by the nuns, to whom she had been very helpful. Of course, no one knew that we were Jewish. But they also had something to hide. They were teaching children, which was forbidden. There were no functioning schools under the occupation. The children of inferior races, such as the Slavs, were not to be educated. So the aura of secrecy, hiding our books when visitors came, worrying about inspections by German patrols, fit well with what I was used to.

The estate we were housed in had a large dining room with a long baronial table. Perhaps it had actually been the kitchen or the servants' food preparation room, since there was a large sink on one wall and shelves all around. I remember how beautiful all the heavy dark oak furniture was, as if from medieval times. The adjoining large room was our dormitory; perhaps it had originally been a sitting room. Now, it had rows of beds along the wall. Since there was no running water, buckets of water brought in from the well stood by the sink, where we also washed and brushed our teeth. There were no bathrooms in use, only an outhouse, a little way from the house, scary to have to use at night.

All the girls were housed in that one dormitory room, perhaps twenty of us, aged eight to sixteen. The nuns all lived upstairs and we never went to their quarters. Mother Superior had an office in a large, well-apportioned room downstairs, where one only went to be chastised for some misdemeanor. Food was served at the long table; then, we had chores—cleaning up, helping with food preparation, and the like. One nun would supervise our meals, but they did not eat with us. For reason of religiously imposed modesty, we understood that the nuns were not supposed to be seen eating. This presented a great challenge. We would begin to complain about some aspect of the food, everyone joining in and the only way for the supervising sister to test the truth of what we were saying was to taste the food. Once we had seen her put a spoonful in her mouth, we had triumphed.

The most common food was oatmeal, a kind of gruel for breakfast, that always seemed to have some unpleasantly textured bits or husks that needed to be removed from the tongue, a source of complaints to be checked. And turnip soup—"No, not turnip soup again"—that often did not taste right, for some thought-up reason.

There was a separate chapel on the grounds, a beautiful stone building, cool, smelling of incense and flowers. I was quite ready to be religious; it seemed to provide comfort and assurance, and the refuge of the chapel was inviting. After the chaos of our lives, it made reassuring sense to be with these women, who all seemed to know their place, to be happy with their assigned tasks, to believe in something. I think there was not a girl in that place who did not want to become a nun.

The nuns were Ursulines, a teaching order. They were divided into gray nuns and blue nuns by the color of their habits. It took me a while to understand that this was a class distinction. The gray nuns were our teachers; the blue nuns did the housework. I was still an odd child and for some reason it was easier for me to make friends with the blue nuns, as I helped in chores, while I was shy among the gray nuns, although I was a good student and always did well in my classes. The blue nuns were called by first names, usually saints' names they must have chosen, Sister Theresa, or Sister Francisca. The gray nuns had last names: Sister Piotrkowsa or Sister Lubinska.

It was obvious that their tasks had to do with their educational level. Gray nuns had higher education, and were from an urban population; the blue nuns were peasant girls who had little or no schooling. Each nun wore a cross hanging from her neck, but what bothered my sense of fairness was that the gray nuns wore their cross on a chain, while the blue nuns' cross hung from a piece of ordinary rope. When I asked one of the teaching nuns about it, using the ideas I was being taught ("Are they not the same in the eyes of God?"), my question was not well received. I had to be more careful, so as not to be labeled a troublemaker.

I later found that there was another reason for the distinctions. The gray nuns brought a dowry to the convent from their well-to-do families; the blue nuns were more like charity cases admitted to the comfort of the convent. Along the way, I had many more disillusion-ments with the religious system. But I fit in as best I could, glad that I had been baptized and had my first communion and could even brag about having had my last rites. No one could question that I was a good Catholic.

Still, I did not really make any friends. I had to be careful and could give only superficial information about who I was and where I was coming from. Not the way to make friends easily at that age, no sharing of secrets here. My mother came to visit me every week; on the first visit, she pointed out one of the girls to me, a dark-haired girl a year younger than I was and well-developed for her age.

"She is Jewish," Genia said. "I know her mother, but I don't know what happened to her parents, they may have been able to leave Poland." I kept all that a secret. Hanka never had any visitors, and I felt very sorry for her. She was super-religious and clung to the nuns. She was not much fun. I did make one friend, Basia, who was bright and energetic. Her parents never appeared. She had an aunt who visited her occasionally, more to check on her than because she was a close or caring relative. It was obvious to me that Basia was not Jewish and yet had some secrets she was covering up. She had an independence that I respected, and we spent a lot of time together.

As long as I can remember, I had had trouble going to sleep. Since I was an only child and spent a lot of time with adults, my bedtime was not very rigidly adhered to. After I learned how to read, I would sneak a book and a flashlight to bed and read. Often, I just daydreamed. I liked that time in bed with the house quiet. It was my time and I did not mind not being asleep. Sleeping in a large room with many girls, it was hard to quiet down. There was no reading because there was no available light, so I would tell stories, plots of books I had read or stories that I made up. Everyone seemed to like it, and often one of the girls would ask me to start telling a story. I made up fairy tales and got quite involved in working out how the story would end, only to discover that, by the time I finished, everyone was asleep.

Part of not sleeping well was that I had a weak bladder, and would sometimes wet my bed, which meant having to go through complicated maneuvers to try to dry the sheet and switch it around the mattress so that it would not be discovered in the morning. As the winter progressed, having to use the outhouse at night was almost unthinkable. It was a hard winter. Going to the outhouse meant plowing through a couple of feet of snow, only to be exposed to freezing temperatures. Even when I ventured out, I often found it difficult to make it in time. Running through the snow and ice with my hands holding on to the crotch of my pajama pants, trying to hold off the stream of urine, was very unpleasant, but it may have had some benefit. That winter most children, in spite of warm gloves and possibly due to malnutrition, suffered from frost-bite on their hands. I never got frostbite and read somewhere that an application of urine prevents frostbite.

But there was an easier solution that I finally took, peeing in the dining room sink. It was just one room away from the bedroom. I could make sure everyone was asleep and quietly tiptoe to the next room, lift myself over the sink, and try to direct the stream so it was as quiet as possible. That was what I finally began doing. But it remained one of the things that stuck in my mind as something that I always will be ashamed of. One day, one of the girls announced that someone had been peeing in the sink at night. There were horrified exclamations of outrage. I joined in the disapproval. Someone suggested a possible culprit; she had not been definitely identified but her identity was suggested. She denied it vigorously; we all refused to believe her denials. I joined in. I was terrified that I might be found out and I stopped the practice. I felt very guilty to have let someone else take the blame. I have never forgotten the incident, and even much later found excuses: it was possible that I was not the only one, maybe the suspect did it too. Maybe if I had admitted to it she never would and we would have exchanged roles. Well, there it was, a sign of cowardice. I had a hard time forgiving myself.

Cesia came often to attend to sick Sisters or children, or to attend some church event. She was invited to be there when the novice nuns took their vows in a beautiful church ceremony. She used to wear a certain kind of perfume with the scent of lilacs in it, the scent I tried to duplicate in my failed attempt to make perfume for my mother's birthday present. But I could always smell her perfume when she had been there, even if she had already left. Somehow, smelling her presence in this setting always made me feel good.

There was one major drama during these first months in the convent. We began to have frequent inspections by the SS in an attempt to stop any possible violation of rules against schooling. Books had to be hidden, classes disrupted when someone came running in to say that a German car was entering the grounds. Often, the nun who intercepted these inspections and tried to delay them would be Sister Brigitte, our French teacher. She was young and attractive and besides fluent French, she also spoke German. She was not a novice; she had taken her final vows and became a bride of Christ. Her hair was shorn under her cap and the convent would be her final home. So it was a shock and a strange surprise when the German inspections increased but it seemed that the SS officer in charge was not trying to uncover illegal activity; rather, he simply wanted to see Sister Brigitte. A month later, it was official, everyone heard that Sister Brigitte was leaving the convent with her officer. We were not allowed to go out, but hung out the windows. Sister Brigitte left, sitting next to the handsome SS officer in an open car. We tried to decipher her expression. Did she look embarrassed or triumphant, sorry or relieved? It was a strange scene that left us very confused. We liked Sister Brigitte—she was fun and brightened up the place.

Besides a concern with not interrupting my education, so she always found classes or schools for me, Genia was determined that I should have my teeth straightened. I was rather buck-toothed and the children nicknamed me rabbit, partly because our Aryan name had the word rabbit (*Krolik*) in it, but partly due to my buck teeth. Already, in the ghetto, Genia had found a dentist and began the task of having braces made for my teeth, but it did not last long and we had to stop. So here we were again. Cesia found a dentist in a nearby town and Genia put together some leftover jewelry she had. The braces had to be made of gold; there was no other metal available. I think I might have already had pieces of my old braces, which were gold. All this was given to the dentist, and Cesia would come to pick me up from the convent and take me to the next town for a fitting.

It was February of 1945 and I was on one of those trips with Cesia to see the dentist, when the front begun to advance. The Russians were no closer than when we had left Warsaw four months previously. The German presence was felt less and less, and there were rumors of people coming into contact with the Russian army, getting supplies, waiting for the end.

It was a cold and hungry winter, and when Cesia came to pick me up, she usually brought some food for us to eat on the bus, on the way to the dentist's office. I looked forward to this trip, though not necessarily to the dentist. This time, there was a sense of urgency in the towns we went through, and people were talking about the advancing front. The dentist visit over, my braces properly adjusted, we came on the street to discover that the buses had stopped running. It was about an hour's ride back to the convent. There was no transportation; we walked some, tried to hitch with passing vehicles, mainly horse-drawn wagons, got some short-distance lifts, walked some more, and finally arrived back late, long after we were expected.

When we got back, Genia and Jasio were waiting for us. They were frantic about our absence. They had taken a train to town, but the trains were no longer running. Genia said she met a man who was leading a horse and said the Russians gave it to him, and that he had been behind the front lines. My mother and Jasio had come because they knew that the front lines were advancing and Genia did not want us to be separated, not knowing exactly what would happen. They stayed overnight at the nunnery. There was no choice but to put them up, and the next morning the three of us started out for our village. The problem was that no one knew the way. They had come on the train, so they knew that the railroad tracks would take us back. But the railroads were the main lines of German retreat and resupply, and were heavily strafed. Small Russian planes would dip down along the tracks and shoot at anything that moved. It seemed like all the German anti-aircraft defenses were gone. We moved along the railroad tracks, and when we heard the approaching aircraft would jump into ditches at the sides of the track and flatten out.

It was very cold. Genia kept telling me not to worry because my hat was made of red wool and when the Russians saw my red hat they would never shoot. I half believed her, half thought she was just trying to keep our spirits up. Jasio, who always had a morose streak, worried that the Germans would stop us and think we were Russian spies. A reprise of what happened to his father in the First World War: he was crossing the front lines to get to the hospital where his wife was giving birth and was taken for a German spy and sent to Siberia for five years.

It took many cold hours, but by the early afternoon we arrived in our village. The Germans were setting up defense lines along the perimeters of the town. An anti-artillery gun was set up in the town square. The town was ready to be defended.

A German soldier came to the door looking for my mother. Lieutenant S. wanted to see her at the barracks; he had some things for her.

When we all still lived with the farmers, before I went to the convent, but other people were already gone, a German patrol came to the house to check everyone's documents. Two soldiers and a Lieutenant. They asked everyone to line up. We did, first the farmer's family, then my mother, then I, then Jasio, the most vulnerable. The two enlisted men started down the line; the Lieutenant hung back observing us. As they checked the families' papers that were being handed to them one by one and handed them back, they came to my mother. As she reached for her (not useful) documents, the Lieutenant stepped forward and motioned them off. "That's enough," he said, "Everyone here is fine," and led them out of the house.

He came back again and asked her to come to the barracks. Jasio insisted on accompanying her; they went and the officer gave her some blankets. She had to be careful not to offend him and not to cause suspicion among the Poles. It was touchy. I don't know if she saw him again after that, but this time Jasio went with her and he loaded them up with more blankets and some foodstuff.

That night, we went to bed waiting to hear the guns go off. The front was coming this way. But there was not a sound all night. Not a shot had been fired. In the morning, we went out to look around. The fortifications were still there where they had stood the night before. The Germans were gone; the Russians were marching in.

As the Russian divisions moved through the town, the marching columns always sang. This was true wherever we were, as the armies moved across Poland by the end of April and the real end of the war, some still moving west, others heading back east. It was not ordinary army singing, more melodic than the marching songs I was used to, or the Germanic barking of aggression. There would usually be a solo voice rising from within the marching throng, harmonizing or singing a stanza; the whole group would then pick up the chorus. It was great to hear, and people hung out of their doorways and windows to listen.

It was a sad, tired-looking, rag-tag army, compared to the well-equipped Germans in their pressed uniforms and shined shoes and mechanized transport. What I remember most are the shoes of the soldiers. They had clearly come on foot over long distances. Their boots were often stuffed with newspapers peeping out of the broken soles and torn tops. It must have indeed been a hard winter's campaign. They were strikingly young, sixteen-, seventeen-, eighteen-year-old country boys. They must have been the last recruits to fight the retreating Germans.

Later in the city, I heard many stories making fun of their lack of sophistication, not knowing how a watch worked, stealing women's nightgowns to take home to their girlfriends, thinking they were fancy wedding dresses. But in the countryside where we were, these could have been the local peasant boys. It was clear that such surroundings were familiar to them. There was enough similarity between the two Slavic languages to make communication easy.

That first day, patrols of three or four soldiers were sent to every house just to make sure that there were no retreating Germans hiding there. When a small group came to the house and saw the store of potatoes, their eyes lit up. They were hungry. They asked the woman in the house if she would make a pot of potatoes cooked in bacon fat. They would come back soon. They had been sleeping in the fields, having nothing but dry army rations. Potatoes cooked in fat with maybe an onion thrown in would have been a great delicacy, a touch of home. We all got busy peeling the potatoes and making a fire. A big pot was filled with cut-up potatoes and tried out fat and the cooking began.

The young soldiers soon returned with more friends. They sat around the kitchen warming themselves near the fire, inhaling the smell of the cooking bacon fat and telling stories of their hardships, waiting for the potatoes to be done. In less than half an hour, another soldier arrived with a message that they would be moving out presently and needed to reassemble.

"No," they said, "we can't leave, the potatoes are not done yet. Just a little longer."

Five minutes later, two more comrades came, this time accompanied by a sergeant. "Everyone is to leave, this is an order. We are moving on."

The women offered to pack up the almost cooked potatoes so they could be taken along. The officer scoffed at the very idea. This was an army, not a bunch of hungry kids. As they started to file out, the youngest of them lingered on, trying the potatoes for tenderness. The sergeant had enough. "If you are not out of here immediately," he said, "you will be charged with desertion."

The young soldier burst out crying. He was still sobbing as two of his friends grabbed him under his arms and dragged him away with them.

I knew just how he felt.

11. Spring 1945: Return to the Convent

The war was over. The death sentence was lifted. If this was freedom, I think many had lost the meaning of that word. At least for me, the habitual behavior of caution, not telling the truth, distrust of strangers, and preserving a cover had become who I was. I did not know how to act otherwise. I certainly did not want to be exposed as a Jew among my schoolmates or the nuns.

So I went back, accompanied by Aunt Cesia, and promises were made that Genia would pay the back tuition that I knew she owed and would quickly find paid work so that she could continue paying for my keep. There were signs of fighting and destruction everywhere now, even in the small towns as the front lines had passed through them. There was war debris everywhere, abandoned burned-out vehicles, broken guns, all the useless objects that a retreating army leaves behind. The clothing and blankets were quickly gathered and put to use. There was a concern that some German soldiers had shed their uniforms and run off into the forest to avoid capture, posing a deadly threat to anyone who might be walking through the woods.

The items that most fascinated me and my friends were abandoned machine gun belts with leftover bullets. My friend Basia and I gathered these, hiding them in our coat pockets, having discovered that the bullets could be opened and were filled with what looked like thin slivers of metal. Little squares, the size of a large fingernail, that if lit would quickly explode with a satisfying pop, a flare-up and an exciting smell of sulphur. The devil's smell. This was wonderful fun when no one could see us.

The large baronial dining table in the room that adjoined our dormitory was perfect for this. We would get up after dark, when we were supposed to have retired for the night, sit around the table and pick up each little square by its corner, light a match to it, and quickly drop it before it could burn our fingers. There was just enough time for it to flash, burn out, and drop on the table surface, faintly glowing. Sometime later, we noticed that the table was becoming marred with little burn marks all over. I don't remember anyone ever discovering it or rebuking us.

Thinking back to the convent experience, I realize that one of the advantages of being among nuns was their own reticence and expectation of privacy. None of us had ever seen any of the sisters without their habits, headdresses, or in any kind of disarray. This meant that after they retired, they could not appear—except, I suppose, in a dire emergency—thus we could count on no supervision at night.

The owners of the baronial mansion in which we were housed must have avoided having it requisitioned by the Germans by providing it to the convent. While our use of it caused minimal damage and probably protected the family art and heirlooms that might have been carted away by the Germans, had they been stationed there, it was not without its hazards. That spring, excited about making a vegetable garden, and clearing some weeds to help the sisters who were going to plant it, we found hidden in the bushes a small red convertible, a beautiful little car, well camouflaged among the overgrowth. It was a two-seater, and made a wonderful play hiding place. Better still, the seats were covered with the softest red leather we had ever seen. We were always on the lookout for materials to make things for our dolls. Toys were very scarce; one was lucky to have a doll or a teddy bear to sleep with. All I had was a little porcelain doll with articulating arms and legs, no more than six inches tall, with very little to wear. The red leather, discarded as it seemed to be in the bushes, was very tempting material. Several of us came back with small manicure scissors with which we cut out squares of the seat covering to bring back and sew into things our dolls needed. Mine got a wonderful little pocketbook on a string, in which she could hide small treasures, and a pair of matching slippers. Again, I don't remember any consequences. Perhaps the nuns did not really pay much attention to us. Having the children there was not their usual occupation, but just a wartime need. They were a teaching order, but perhaps not really caretakers. Maybe in those extreme times, children were given more privacy than is the norm now.

It was confusing not to know what to expect of the ending of the war. Life went back to normal. But what was normal? Our families were gone, our homes destroyed. Some parents appeared and collected their daughters. No one came for the little girl, Hanka, who I knew from my mother was Jewish. I wanted to talk to her, thinking she might need comforting, but did not quite dare yet. She was, as I remember, the most devout of the girls, very attached to one of sisters and talking about becoming a nun. In all this terror and confusion of war, life in the convent looked very attractive. There was stability and community and respect that one could count on even from the enemy. They had good times too, working together, praying together, singing, doing chores, and looking forward to a secure future. Sometimes, members of the male clergy would come to stay and there was much fluster of preparing food and rooms, and general excitement. One bishop was particularly jolly. He played the piano, a glass of spirits always on the sideboard, and we could hear the nuns laughing and vying to bring him what he needed. There was definitely an attraction to that life for the girls.

It was the first time in my life that I thought about belonging to a group, as opposed to making sure that I was not identified with one, at the cost of my life. I could actually choose a religion. There were many questions to be asked, and now I could ask them.

It was a difficult time. The adults were busy trying to find which of their family or friends had survived. Jasio went to Wloclawek to see what had become of his parents' house, my grandparents' house. At the beginning of the war, my grandfather had gathered all the family valuables, maybe after a German decree that Jews had to turn all those over to the Gestapo. He had them buried in a small iron box somewhere in back of their house, not on their land. He thought that might be too obvious. He had sent a map to Jasio and Genia showing how to find the buried treasure. Jasio was very anxious to get there and start digging. I am not sure if he still had the actual map or was working from memory. He hired men to help him dig and hired other men to watch over the digging. It turned out that new construction was going on in the area of the plot. Genia had not much hope that anything would be found, but Jasio, ever the optimist, was counting on it and would not give up.

Aunt Cesia knew she had lost everyone but us, her niece and nephew and grandniece—me. She had a younger brother who had emigrated to America when he was eighteen, not heard from much after that. People encouraged her and my mother to try to locate him, but Genia said that since he had made no effort to find his sister all through the war and after, she was not inclined to look for him. She was corresponding with Mietek through the Red Cross as well as their friends in Switzerland. He was currently living in London, and had a job offer from the United States.

It was a beautiful spring. As the leaves and flowers begun to unfurl, it was a symbolic unfurling of years of held-in emotions and terror. For me, not much had changed. I was not sure what I had to look forward to, but I began to feel free to ask questions, to look at my feelings, to think of my own future. I still did not dare to utter the word "Jew"; for many years afterwards, if anyone asked me if I was Jewish, way into my adulthood, my immediate response was an emphatic "No." I wanted to tell my friend Basia, and not being able quite to say it, hinted to her about a past where I had lived in Warsaw behind a wall, till I saw that she understood. But neither of us had the nerve yet to say the words out loud.

Basia and I started to plan our futures. She had always wanted to be a veterinarian. I was going to be a doctor, like my aunt Cesia, but we would practice in the countryside, bringing our skills to the peasants. She would take care of the horses, pigs, and cows, and I would help the people. We would travel by motorcycle all around the country, helping.

Now that the war was over, the estate that had been given over to the convent was to be returned to its original owners. We were to move to the city, perhaps to what had been the original building of the order, requisitioned in turn by the authorities for some administrative city use. We were to move to Lodz, and eventually go to the newly organized public schools. But, for now, we could stay on the beautiful estate grounds till the end of May. In anticipation of the move, Genia began to look for work in Lodz, and to look for a place to live there. Housing was very difficult to find, as so many streamed back to the city. It was also difficult for her, getting ready to part with the farm family, of whom she had become very fond.

The estate had its own chapel, which became my favorite place at Easter. Dark and cool, it smelled of incense and flowers. In anticipation of Easter and its celebration, a pallet was laid out, surrounded by flowers, with a figure of crucified Christ upon it. While the dead body of Christ was laid out in chapel, there had to be attendants at all times. Some of the nuns took turns sitting there, as did the girls. It was my favorite thing to do. I volunteered for vigil all the time, and stayed till late into the night. I had not had a chance to mourn for any of the many dead in my life. Here with the quiet, and the smell of flowers and incense, I mourned with my whole heart for the crucified God.

The month of May is a month dedicated to Mary, when nightly vespers are obligatory to pray to the Holy Virgin. As much as I liked the inside of the chapel, I liked the outdoors more that month. Flowers were in bloom. The best part of it was that, as everyone went into the chapel for vespers, I had those hours to myself, to wander about, and I thought, "I adore God's creation just as it is happening." That is what I told Mother Superior when called in to answer to the transgression of not attending vespers. I argued that I was, in fact, worshipping God directly, in full appreciation of His power, looking at every leaf and flower, listening to the birds, appreciating the nature of everything. Thus my contact with God was more direct and more sincere. My argument, which I thought was very persuasive, was not well received. My transgression was not about religious feelings, I realized; it was about obedience. It was not until years later, when I studied religion in college, that I realized that I was, in fact, making the Protestant argument.

I felt myself to be very religious, and I wondered if I was sinning in not telling of my previous deception. Should this be something to mention in confession, to which we went every week? I approached Hanka, who still had not heard from her family, and told her not to feel alone, as I was Jewish too and knew about her. It seemed that, in her own religious fervor, she had already confessed this sin. Soon after,

I started to have a feeling that she confessed about me as well. I was annoyed at myself for having spoken to her. But she assured me that it was only in confession and thus had to be kept secret by the priest. Yet I thought there was a subtle change of attitude towards me. Was this another disappointment, that the secrecy of the confessional was not respected?

I never really found out, because not long afterward, the new civil authorities announced that schools would reopen that September. All during the six years of occupation, public schools were closed; the Germans very deliberately did not want to educate the conquered, or allow the student setting to be a possible center of opposition. Now, all these young people had somehow to be moved forward in their lives. Of course, many had been taught, as I had, in surreptitious, illegal underground schools, or simply at home. So placement tests were to be given; the youngsters would be assigned to a grade according to the results.

The move to Lodz happened shortly before the date for the placement tests; on that date, I was informed that I would not be allowed to take the bus to town for the test. I was dumbfounded. The decision came from Mother Superior. She had said that I was "uppity" enough as it was, that undoubtedly were I to take the test I would be advanced one or two grades, which would add to my sense of superiority. It was her duty to save me from the deadly sin of pride. She could not be a party to that.

Well, of course I would be advanced—that was the whole purpose of taking the test. I have often thought that her attitude had to do with knowing that I was Jewish. When the city bus stopped by the convent to pick up girls for the test, I walked out the gate and hurried a few blocks ahead to catch it there, where I would not be seen or stopped. I took the test and was placed two grades ahead of my age average.

When I returned to the convent late that afternoon, I was aware I had done something unthinkable, disobeying a directive from Mother Superior. Sister Lubinska, who had always been my friend, seemed genuinely distressed. She told me that my only choice was to beg for forgiveness. I was to go to the Mother Superior, kneel down before her, and kiss her hand, while promising never to disobey like that again. I froze. I simply could not do it. Not because I was too proud to go through the motions—it was because it would have been so insincere. I could have gotten down on my knees and begged her for anything, if it was something I wanted. But I was very proud of myself, that I had gone into town on my own and taken the test, and I knew I did well. I was not sorry. In fact, the only answer I missed was when I was asked who was the President of the United States. I said Roosevelt. No, I was told, he had died; it was Harry Truman. Such news did not reach us in the convent.

My mother was called in the next day and told that I could not stay any longer. I was obstinate and disobedient, and not the right kind of child for them. They were sorry because of my Aunt Cesia, who had been such a help to the Sisters. But given my mother's difficulty in paying my fees, perhaps it would be best if she removed me from the convent as soon as possible. I think I packed my few things and left the next day. Except for Basia, with whom I remained in contact, there was no one there I missed. I would be living with my mother again and that alone made me very happy.

12. Living with Genia in Lodz

My mother had secured a position as a secretary to the regional minister of the interior. With the position came an assignment of very-hard-to-get living quarters. It was just a large room into which we could fit two beds, with a shared bathroom and a kitchen, rarely used, down the hall. This was an old apartment building that was heated by coal. There was a hearth in each apartment and a tile chimney running through the building, which would hold the heat. We had our own supply of coal, which we laid at night and fired up in the morning. It would heat up quickly, but in the winter these early mornings were terribly cold. Any water standing in the room would be frozen; until the tile chimney heated up, it was best to stay under the covers. I don't remember ever carrying the ashes away. I think they could be shaken down through an open flue to the basement.

The school I went to was almost directly across the street. This meant that I always thought I had enough time to get there and was often late. My mother would tell me it was time to get up, but I would burrow deeper under the covers and often fall asleep, dreaming that I was getting ready for school. When I woke up to her urgent shakings, I was really surprised that I was not fully dressed and ready to go. Many of my daydreams that winter had to do with having some kind of a warm coach that would take me to school while I still slept. We had a basin of water for washing up in the room, never quite warm enough. Breakfast was just a piece of bread and some tea. Then, a second breakfast, as it was called, brought in from home, which for me was usually a buttered roll with a piece of chocolate for a filling. A late lunch was served in the school, which was a bigger warm meal. As per usual custom, the midday meal was larger and served by the workplace or school. There was usually a long lunch break, so my mother's work ended late. Often she would not be home till late, sometimes when I was already in bed. I liked to read in bed, which helped me to stay up till she got home. I always had trouble falling asleep but liked that quiet time when I could read as long as I wanted. That partly accounted for my difficulty in getting up in the morning.

Supper I usually ate out by myself. I rather liked that; it made me feel very grown up. Due to limited living situations, people who were lucky enough to have large apartments, or perhaps were in their prewar quarters, set up food service places in their homes, serving paid dinner. There was one I usually went to; they knew me there and I paid with money that Genia left with me for dinner. That was most of the time, especially in the winter. Their houses would be warm and there would be hot soup. When the weather got warm, I sometimes, very guiltily, took my dinner money and went to a café that served ice cream. Ice cream was an unbelievable luxury. It is hard to believe now, but a big dish of ice cream with whipped cream and a cherry or some strawberry jam on top cost exactly the same as my whole supper would have. It was money well spent—it made me feel luxurious, naughty, and wealthy, and just as sated as if I had eaten a whole meal of noodles, soup, or whatever I might have been served in someone's apartment. Since most of my friends had to go home for supper, I felt very privileged and grown up to be able to make this choice to treat myself.

Tuesday was market day in Lodz, and I had a friend I could always talk into going with me to the market during the long lunch break. Sometimes, we would not go back to school but play hooky, wandering through the market looking at the geese and chickens that the farmers brought and sucking on pickles bought out of a large barrel, which was the only thing we had enough money for that was immediately edible.

Thinking back, this was a very odd time for me. I was out of immediate danger but in a strange kind of limbo. The excitement of daily survival with Genia and Jasio was no longer there. It seemed that they each had their own things to do. Mine was to go to school, which was not very interesting—easy for me, but it had no direction. I still lived in my old identity under my war-assumed name, as did my mother. We, at least I, did not dare tell anyone we were Jewish, but in a way it was not relevant. Except for the German definition, we never felt Jewish. It had no place in our lives; there was no community to belong to and the family for whose sake my mother kept the few traditions she followed was gone. I think I was very lonely and depressed, but it certainly was not something I recognized at the time.

Years later, when talking with a sensitive friend about feelings of depression and helplessness, I told her I felt as if I was standing on the edge of a great abyss trying not to fall in. She suddenly asked me, "How old are you?" And without hesitating, I said "twelve." Later, I looked at a picture of me from that year that was on my school bus ID and I was shocked to see the most depressed little girl I had ever seen. Yet my memory of the time is of those presumably exciting highlights of eating, cutting school, wandering around town, finding things to do by myself. Once I went to see a movie, but forgot my glasses, which I only wore to school. I had to sit in the front row and kept asking the friend I went with what was happening till she got annoyed with me. The problem was reading the subtitles, which I could not see. It was an American film called, I think, *The Gray Lord*; I never found it again.

I don't think I had many friends. The adults around swirled with plans, but I had no idea what we would do.

Jasio, who had gone to Wloclawek to try to regain his parents' house and factory and find the jewelry that his father hid, came back having rented the house, thus having a small monthly income but without finding any valuables. He found Marysia, who was nineteen, originally from Wloclawek. Marysia went there to see if she could find any surviving family. She found no one. He offered to help her.

Now, Jasio was in love, and he and Marysia were going to be married. This was not something that Genia looked upon favorably. Having taken care of him for so long, she had planned to pass him on to one of her friends, who would have been happy to take on a very presentable thirty-year-old. Marysia was more than ten years his junior, with not much to recommend her as a responsible caretaker in Genia's eyes. She was very beautiful and very needy, and Jasio took it upon himself to take care of her. She adored him and he could not do enough for her. She in turn loved being taken care of, something neither my mother nor I respected. Her escape from the Warsaw ghetto as a young teenager and her subsequent survival all had been arranged by a series of smitten admirers. She was used to that.

Genia had some big decisions to make. She loved her job and basked in the energy of the whole country lifting itself from destruction. She was obviously well liked and appreciated in her office. There was a future in the department. There was the excitement of finding old friends who had survived or, having gone east to Russia, were now returning. There was a lot of joy. I tagged along. Once in a while, someone paid attention to me. I remember one time walking down the street with a recently returned friend of both my parents, when I stopped to look in a store window, where some very strange round yellow balls were set in a small basket.

"Do you know what that is?" he asked. I didn't know. "Those are apricots," he said. I had never even heard the word before. He was amused. He went inside and got me one. I bit into it and was rather disappointed, but tried not to show it and thanked him politely.

It seems to me now that perhaps my lack of interaction with the adults had to do with my own reticence and lack of affect. I was very private; I cried in my bed, but never in public. I was never grateful for anything given me, just polite. I can't remember wanting anything very much. It was almost as if I could not be sure what an appropriate emotion would be.

While Genia corresponded with Mietek, it was not clear what had happened to my father. I used to have dreams about him, that he would be returning and I would run to him, but he would disappear or a car would come and I had to get out of the way. Then, once during that year, I overheard Genia having a conversation in the hallway of our house with someone she met. She was being told that Bolek, my father, had died in Vilno, one of those areas that changed hands, from Russians to Germans and back again. He had been arrested by the German authorities and was in jail when the Russian army moved in and opened up the prisons. Whether he did not leave fast enough or went in the wrong direction, back towards Poland, the area was retaken by Germany and he was again arrested and died. I guess he was shot.

I did not know what to do with the information. It had no effect on me. I thought I should cry, but I couldn't. I wanted to tell my mother that I overheard the conversation, but felt if I did that, I should have an appropriate reaction. But I felt nothing. So I started telling myself some sad stories, sad fairy tales, to make myself cry so I could appear in front of her. Nothing happened, so I gave up. I never told her that I overheard the conversation, and she never told me.

Years later, after my mother died, I found among the letters she had saved one that was written in my exact handwriting. My handwriting is quite distinctive in its sloppiness, something I always assumed had to do with my lack of early schooling. But the stamped date on the envelope was 1943. Inside was a letter from my father, written when I was in the pseudo-orphanage. He asked if Genia had been to visit me and to please tell him how I was.

I cried and cried when I read that, and it makes me cry today. The similarity of the handwriting is one those strange things I cannot explain.

A time came when Genia found herself in a very difficult conflict. I don't know how much was explained to me, but the tension was clear. I heard her talking about it to her friends. Mietek was now on his way to the United States, where he had been offered a job because of engineering contacts he had made during his stay in South America. He wanted her to come and join him. She was happy in Poland, she liked her job, and she had around her the friends who had survived the war. They had a shared experience; they all understood what had happened. She had not seen her husband for seven years. They had only been married for a little over a year before then. He was a difficult man, as everyone reminded her. Was she the same woman she was when they separated? How different had his experiences been from hers, over those seven years?

She was finally free, independent, and needed by the country. I know she asked everyone for advice. I know that I was very lost. I thought we would leave; it made no sense to try to make a life for myself, even if I could do that now. I started cutting school more and more, and my grades went down. I made no friends. What was the point? I would only lose them again. Genia was one of the few among her friends who looked at the future of Poland with optimism. Most were looking for ways to get away. There was clearly still anti-Semitism. News of pogroms in other parts of country, violence against the returning Jews, especially if they claimed their property, was not advertised, but was whispered about. It was clear that one should not advertise one's Jewish past. It was not clear to me who I was to be. I did not know any Jewish children my age and, anyway, I had never felt any affinity with them.

Most of Genia's friends were advising her to leave. What an opportunity, to go to America and be with her husband! And what of her marriage vows?

A relative of my father's who had been a long-time Communist activist was now in Poland in an important position in the Ministry of Justice. Genia had always respected him and he liked her. She went to speak with him. He was committed to the new Poland, but saw the problems of the rising Communist regime and was reluctant to advise her to stay. He laid out both sides and finally said, "Why don't you go, and if you don't like it you can always come back?"

I remember these words because they were what finally convinced her to go, and they have come back to haunt both of us through the years. It seems that turning back is never as easy as it seems.

Finally, I was presented as the reason to go. "If you don't want to go," said her friends, "think of Krysia, would you deprive her of that opportunity? You owe it to her to go."

I think by that time I had very little to keep me there. I was letting school go. I had always been a very good student—proud of it and taking pleasure in it—but what did it matter? I would not be there anyway. I let all my friends go or did not try to make new ones. What was the point of it? Just more losses. My mother hired a tutor to give me English lessons. I started to learn English and to look at a future of passing again with a new identity. It was comfortingly familiar. The idea that appealed to me was the unknown of that new future. Everything here was dead and flat.

A few prewar friends of Genia and Mietek told me that Mietek was a very difficult person. I should be patient when I got there, and try to please him. So I sat down and wrote him a letter telling him about myself, trying to explain myself and to open communication. The letter was returned to me with a note saying that he did not read it, because my handwriting was too sloppy for him to bother, and unless I would learn to write more clearly he could not be bothered to read my letters.

What did I do? I don't remember. I think I wrote a few neat, polite notes.

The next few months were taken up with the final formalities of documents. Genia had to go back to her married name, but I had never been legally adopted by Mietek. Getting a visa to go to the United States if I was not his daughter would have created complications. The advantage of the war was that documents could be declared lost, so my name was simply changed again. I was now Kristine Krol, a name I had never used before. I went back to my father's last name after the war (on my school bus pass it appears hyphenated with my Aryan wartime name, creating a comfortable transition of identities), but now it was simply taken off, never to be used again. I must not use it now, because it would undermine the legal myth of my being Mietek's legal child and possibly jeopardize our entry to the United States.

In June of 1946, we took a train to Gdansk and then a ferry to Sweden. Immigration directly to the United States was not possible at the time. One had to wait for a quota, usually for years. Sweden and Canada were two of the countries that allowed immigrants to come and wait there for their US quota. Mietek had assured my mother that he would be able to make arrangements for her to leave Sweden very soon. How that came about is another story, but we were only there for six weeks before we got our visas to the States.

Afterword: What is Left???

When I saw the Jewish cemetery in Warsaw in 1972, my first trip to Poland in twenty-six years, it looked just like the overgrown field that stood untilled for thirty years at the side of my house in New Hampshire. The trees were roughly the same age and type. A motley assortment of deciduous saplings leaning over a thick, mossy underbrush. My New Hampshire field was strewn with rocks that once had formed a stone wall, and boulders that, a long time ago, had been moved aside to clear the soil. Here, the moss-covered stones, and what looked like boulders, barely visible in the underbrush, on closer inspection were recognizable as broken and overturned gravestones.

Some had been overturned by the emerging roots of the newly grown trees. Others had been deliberately broken, their inscriptions barely visible, a name here, a date there, the Hebrew lettering on some faded to what looked like an accidental scrape.

It was June. My mother had died that April. Mietek, my stepfather, had asked me to accompany him on his first trip back to Poland since he had left the country as a young soldier in 1939. I did not want to be alone with him and insisted that my daughter Lisa, who was thirteen at the time, come with us. One of the purposes of Mietek's visit was to go to the grave of his parents, who had died before the war and were buried at this cemetery.

As I was planning for the trip, my uncle Jasio said: "Mietek will be visiting his parents' grave. Your other grandmother is buried there too. Why don't you see if you can find her grave?" This was my real father's mother. Since we had come to America and were reunited with Mietek, we never spoke of that part of the family. There was a pretense that I had no other father. He liked it when, on rare occasions, people who had just met us commented on a family likeness between us.

Mietek and my mother had married when I was five years old, not long after her divorce from my father. A year after the marriage, the war separated them for seven years. With the war over, he found himself in the United States. Since I had never been legally adopted by him, for the sake of simplifying immigration procedures, my mother and I entered America as his wife and daughter, and I simply began to use his name. By the age of twelve, I had already lived under three different surnames for different purposes, so adopting one more for immigration seemed commonplace.

My parents had not lived together since I was three years old and my father had been killed during the war, sometime, somewhere, caught in the moving eastern front in the early years of the war, between German incursions from the west and Russian incursions from the east. Mietek did not like to acknowledge that my father had ever existed. Once Mietek and my mother were together, my father was never mentioned.

Jasio told me that my father's mother's name was Balbina Dywan, and that she had killed herself a year before the war began by jumping from a two-story window. That is all I know about her to this day. Whether the cause was the darkening political situation (was she a political person?) or her son's failing marriage, or something else, I have no way of ever finding out. But there it was. She was, according to Jasio, buried in the Jewish cemetery in Warsaw. She was my grand-mother, and Jasio thought it would be appropriate for me to put flowers on her grave, if I could find it.

Following the code of silence about my father, which I had been taught to maintain out of fear of Mietek's temper, I did not mention any of this to Mietek. On the way to the cemetery, Mietek asked the taxi to stop at a flower shop and when he bought a bouquet of flowers, I did too. A bunch of pink and white carnations wrapped tightly with a strip of aluminum foil. The cemetery was surrounded by a tall brick wall. We were discharged at the narrow gate, which opened onto a wide alley of the cemetery, with narrower paths running off to the sides. On one side was a small caretaker's building, more like a shack, where one checked in and was expected to leave a contribution towards reclaiming what once had been a well-tended cemetery. There was a new part of large, even ostentatious, graves of those recently deceased who had held some important government rank. The restoration of the old graves had obviously proceeded very slowly. In the shack, there was an elderly caretaker poring over large, crumbling ledgers. He explained to us that his task was to catalogue the graves for which there was a record and to find those whose distant relatives sent funds for their recovery. There was an attempt to create a map of the cemetery. It would take years yet. I gave him my grandmother's name, but the ledgers were organized by years. He asked the date of her death, which might help him place the location, but I did not know the date.

Mietek, who knew exactly where his parents' graves were, was anxious to move on, so we followed him. Lisa and I walked more slowly behind him, and I took quick forays left and right off the main path trying to decipher the names on the stones that were still upright, in some vain hope of finding the name I was looking for. Finally, I could see Mietek stop at a short distance from us. I was not up to asking for his cooperation in what I was doing. I turned to Lisa and said, "Let's keep walking. If we don't find it by the time we catch up with him, we'll just put the flowers on his parents' grave."

I held the bunch of flowers tightly in my hand and suddenly, without my being aware of any movement, the flowers were spilled at my feet. It was the strangest sensation. I had not been aware of either opening my hand or of the moment of the blossoms falling. It was like a break in time. Suddenly, the aluminum wrapping was unfurled and the flowers were on the ground. What happened afterwards was even stranger.

"She must really want those flowers," I heard myself saying to my daughter, with a feeling of assurance that the fall was in direct response to my previous comment. I bent down, gathered the flowers, and with a strange certainty made a right turn on the path, reading the grave-stone names. The third grave from the edge said Balbina Dywan.

This remains one of the strangest events in my life. I was really glad that Lisa was there to witness it. I can bring back the strange feeling of disconnection in time, from walking down the path holding the flowers tightly in my hand to the moment when they were spread in front of my feet. And the strange sense of certainty as I made the right turn off the path and started reading the names. These two feelings have stayed with me. I can recall them easily because they are like no others. Seeing my grandmother's name on the gravestone was at once a complete shock and a sense of affirmation.

I have never forgotten the strange feeling of having both those contradictory perceptions simultaneously.

What has really puzzled me most, accepting what had happened, was the question: *why should she care?* Why should my grandmother, whom I hardly knew and don't remember, care whether I put flowers on her grave forty years after her death?

Is that what is left?

When our lives are over is there still some unsatisfied energy? A desire for continuity? For remembrance? For if this is so, I am writing this book to satisfy that desire. Perhaps there are millions of restless souls who need this homage of memory. Maybe I will be among them. The story is told for them. These were momentous events. There was life and death, horror, suffering, honor and sacrifice, and arbitrary survival. I walked through those times and I would like this book to be an offering to all those who walked there also and fell. An offering to their heirs, real, spiritual, or intellectual. The bouquet of flowers.

Photos and Documents

Grandparents

A formal photo of my grandfather Gershon Lubowski, taken in 1906 to present to his brother who was emigrating to Palestine

My grandmother Helena Fogel, the eldest of eight children whom Helena raised after her mother died when she was 14 years old

Before the War

Author's birth certificate and birth
photo with grandmother, mother
and father. My grandmother has the
worried expression on her face
I remember she always had

In a baby carriage with visiting grandparents, mother, and uncle Jasio in a school uniform, at a park in Warsaw 1934

Myself with mother and grandparents

Myself age five with grandparents in a wool suit my grandmother knit

In the park with mother and grandmother, wearing an ermine coat, my favorite

Age five fooling around in my grandparents' house, wearing grandfather's hat

With my father at my grandparents' house

In the courtyard of grandparents' house in Włocławek, with a cousin, sitting on my grandfather's horse used to pull his delivery wagon

Doorway of grandparents' house with my grandfather and Jasio, holding grandmother's dog

In front of loading dock in Włocławek, with grandmother, dog and holding chicken

Sitting on the factory loading dock with two dogs, a guard dog and a house pet

Genia and Mietek (Krol), first married,1938

My mother and me, studio photos to send to Mietek, 1940

The War Begins

German-issued certificate that house was burned down in the invasion of
September 1939, dated 4 Novemeber 1939. which entitled us to search for new
accommodations

Possible Escape to Italy

KGL. ITALIENISCHE VERTRETUNG
IN WARSCHAU – MONIUSZKI 10

Warschau, den 14 März 1940/XVIII

N° 1102

Dichiarazione

Si dichiara che nulla osta da parte di questa Regia Rappresentanza acché la Signora Eugenia K r ò l con la figlia Cristina Maria Devert si rechi in Italia.

Il visto di ingresso nel Regno le verrà rilasciato su presentazione dei documenti di viaggio tedeschi, nonché di documenti comprovanti la sua origine ariana.

Erklärung

Hiermit wird erklärt dass gegen die Abreise nach Italien des Frau Eugenia K r ò l mit tochter Cristina Maria Devert seitens der hiesigen Italienischen Vertretung nichts einzuwenden ist.

Dieses Einreisevisum wird Ihnen jedoch erst nach Vorlage der unentbehrlichen Reisedokumente, der Bescheinigung seitens der Deutschen Behörder sowie des Nachweises Ihrer arischen Abstammung, erteilt werden.

DER VERTRETERG DER ITALIENISCHEN
INTERESSEN IN WARSCHAU
KGL. BOTSCHAFTSRAT
(M. di Stefano)
i.A.
KGL. BOTSCHAFTS-SEKRETÄR
(G.V. Soro)

A letter of interest in Italian and German, from the Italian Embassy, 14 March 1940

Certificate of Aryan Origin issued by All Saints Church in Warsaw, 22 March 1940 (needed for a visa to Italy)

109/

V e r z e i c h n i s
des Umzugsgutes für KRÓL Eugenia und Kind Krystyna.
----

6 Tag 4 Nachthemden
5 Büstenhalter
6 Reformen,5 Paar Strümpfe
4 Kleider,1 Sommermantel
1 Winterpelzmantel,1 Windbluse
1 Rock,1 Schlafrock
1 Muff,2 Pullover
2 Blusen,2 Kopftücher
1 Regenmantel,1 Handtasche
2 Paar Schuhe,1 P.Gummischuhe
2 Pyjamas,2 Schürzen,1 Trauring
1 Paar Morgenpantoffel,1 Kostüm
1 Jackett mit Pelz,1 Tasche
1 Schaal,1 Paar Handschuhe
1 Alpaccahanduhr
1 Reiseplaid mit Kissem u.Kisschen
1 Welltuch,1 Decke mit 6 Bezügen
je 12 Bezüge f.kissen u.Kisschen
6 Bettlacken,6 Handtücher
3 Badetücher, xxxxxxxxxxx
8 Tischtücher   2 Servietten
le Waschlappen,15 Taschentücher
1 Schirm,3 Gürtel,1 Necessaire
2 Thermosflaschen
1 Nähzeugkästchen,1 Skihose
1 Paar Schuhe
div.Toiletteartickel

f.das Kind

2 Kinderhandtaschen,1 Spielbär
7 Hemden,5 Pyjamas,8 Unterhosen
5 Büstenhalter,5 Paar strümpfe
3 Paar Secken 14 Kleidchen
1 Schlafrock ,1 Regenpelerine
1 Mantel,1 Herbstmantel
2 Blusen,2 Röcke,2 Mützen
1 Blaubluse,1 Jackett
3 Sweater,2 Paar Schuhe,
1 Badehose,1 Raithose,
1 Paar Morgenpantoffel,
div.Haarbänder,Kragen u.Manschetten
1 Peltzkindermantel
div.Toiletteartickel

Hauptzollamt Warschau-West

Eing   22.APR.1940

Anlagen

Krakau den   1940.

VII/Schg/ak

Genehmigungsbescheid.

Hiermit erteile ich KRÓL Eugenia
die devisenrechtliche Genehmigung
zur Mitnahme,des aus nebenstehender
xxxxxxxxxxxx Aufstellung ersicht-
lichen Umzugsgutes in das Ausland.

Die evtl.rot durchgestrichenen
Gegenstände sind von der Mitnahme
ausgeschlossen.

Diese Genehmigung tritt nach 3
Monaten ausser Kraft.

Im Auftrag.

List of items allowed to take when leaving Poland for Italy issued by the Gestapo, 22 April 1940

Genia's new counterfeit ID (birth date and place of birth match the certificate of Aryan origin) provided to the Italian Embassy with visa application documentation, issued 15 March 1940

The Warsaw Ghetto

Just before moving to the Ghetto, 1942

In front of the room we had in the Ghetto apartment. I am wearing the shoes I later traded for a jar of bacon fat

With my mother and Jasio, at the entrance to the ghetto cafe where she worked, located on Ceglana Street

Envelopes of letters from and to Mietek, delivered to the Ghetto and sent to Brazil, censored and stamped by the Gestapo

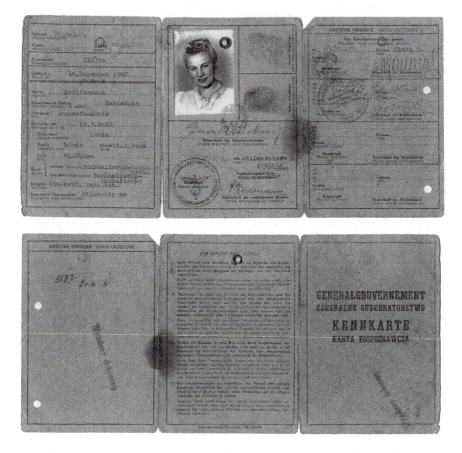

Genia's Ken-Karte, Wartime German-issued ID, December 1942 until December 1947

Outside the Ghetto

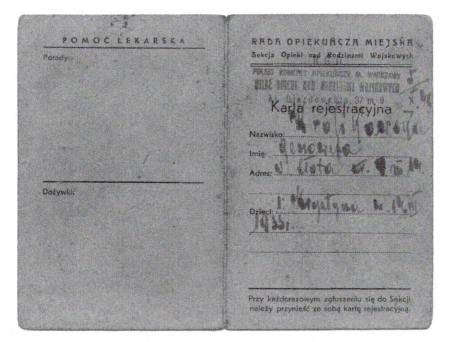

Genowefa and Krystyna Krolikowska registered with the Warsaw Committee for relief to military families, October 1943

First Communion, 1943

Letter from a cousin of Mietek from London, written to me at the Ursuline nuns, Mickiewicza 10, Milanowek pod Warsaw. Checked by the Polish army censors, 8 September 1945

The War is Over

Genia's post war ID as a government employee, issued June 1946 in Lodz

My school bus pass after the war with names; Devert-Krolikowska, issued 15 September 1946 in Lodz

Leaving Poland

My passport photo to leave Poland, 1946

My mother and I in Sweden, on the way to the USA, July 1946

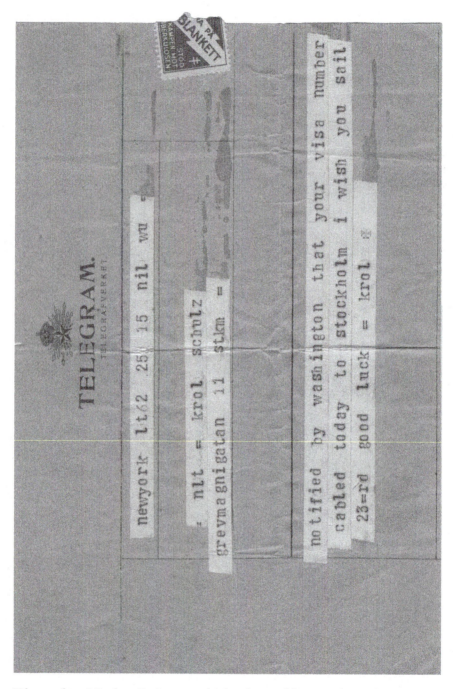

TELEGRAM.
TELEGRAFVERKET.

newyork lt62 25 15 nil wu =

= nlt = krol schulz
grevmagnigatan 11 stkm =

notified by washington that your visa number
cabled today to stockholm i wish you sail
23=rd good luck = krol =

144   Telegram from Mietek to Genia setting the date for travel from Sweden to the USA

Lost Child

POSZUKIWANA

9-cio letnia
MARA MATYLDA MAKOWSKA
córka Jana i Jutty, ur. w roku 1937

Do roku 1941 zamieszkiwała w Warszawie, we wrześniu 1941 przewieziona do Berlina. W maju 1943 wywieziona z Berlina do obozu, dzieci z transportu tego znajdują się prawdopodobnie w jednym z sierocińców.

Rysopis: blondynka, szczupła, twarzyczka szeroka, oczy niebieskie. Załączona fotografia jest z r. 1943.

Ktokolwiek wiedziałby o losie lub miejscu pobytu dziecka, proszony jest zawiadomić Ministerstwo Oświaty, Wydział Opieki nad Dzieckiem (pokój 259) lub Polski Czerwony Krzyż, Warszawa, Piusa 24.

Druk. „Zdobnicza Nowa"   № B-001446

Poln. Militärmission
Berlin-Charlottenburg, Schlüterstr. 42

Research

from **Eugenia Makowska, Warsaw**

for the nine years old

Mara Matylda Makowska

born 7th of Nov. 1937 in Warsaw

Name of the last known foster-parents was **Lebau**. These were imprisoned by the Gestapo in Berlin 1943.

Informations to: **Polish Red Cross**
Berlin-Schlachtensee, Eidesstädter Weg

or to: **Polish Military Mission**
Berlin-Charlottenburg, Schlüterstr. 42

Newspaper ads searching for Mara Matylda Makowska (the little Marie), sent to Germany for safe keeping by her aunt Ana Makowska. She was never found